*easy*

Michael Miller

**que**®
800 East 96th Street
Indianapolis, Indiana 46240

W9-BRZ-878

DISCARDED

# CONTENTS

# EASY FACEBOOK®

ISBN-13: 978-0-7897-5026-6
ISBN-10: 0-7897-5026-0

Library of Congress Cataloging-in-Publication data is on file and available upon request.

Printed in the United States of America

First Printing: October 2012

## TRADEMARKS

## WARNING AND DISCLAIMER

## BULK SALES

Que Publishing offers excellent discounts on this book when ordered in quantity for bulk purchases or special sales. For more information, please contact

U.S. Corporate and Government Sales
1-800-382-3419
corpsales@pearsontechgroup.com

For sales outside of the U.S., please contact

International Sales
international@pearsoned.com

**Editor-in-Chief**
Greg Wiegand

**Acquisitions Editor**
Michelle Newcomb

**Development Editor**
Keith Cline

**Managing Editor**
Kristy Hart

**Senior Project Editor**
Lori Lyons

**Senior Indexer**
Cheryl Lenser

**Technical Editor**
Vince Averello

**Editorial Assistant**
Cindy Teeters

**Interior and Cover Designer**
Anne Jones

**Composition**
TnT Design, Inc.

**Proofreader**
Paula Lowell

## ABOUT THE AUTHOR

**Michael Miller** is a successful and prolific author with a reputation for practical advice, technical accuracy, and an unerring empathy for the needs of his readers.

Mr. Miller has written more than 100 best-selling books over the past two decades. His books for Que include *Facebook for Grown-Ups, Easy Computer Basics, Absolute Beginner's Guide to Computer Basics, My Pinterest,* and *The Ultimate Digital Music Guide.*

He is known for his casual, easy-to-read writing style and his practical, real-world advice—as well as his ability to explain a variety of complex topics to an everyday audience.

You can email Mr. Miller directly at easyfacebook@molehillgroup.com. His website is located at www.molehillgroup.com.

## DEDICATION

To Sherry—it does get easier, doesn't it?

## ACKNOWLEDGMENTS

Thanks to the usual suspects at Que, including but not limited to Greg Wiegand, Michelle Newcomb, Keith Cline, and technical editor Vince Averello.

## WE WANT TO HEAR FROM YOU!

As the reader of this book, *you* are our most important critic and commentator. We value your opinion and want to know what we're doing right, what we could do better, what areas you'd like to see us publish in, and any other words of wisdom you're willing to pass our way.

As an associate publisher for Que Publishing, I welcome your comments. You can email or write me directly to let me know what you did or didn't like about this book—as well as what we can do to make our books better.

*Please note that I cannot help you with technical problems related to the topic of this book. We do have a User Services group, however, where I will forward specific technical questions related to the book.*

When you write, please be sure to include this book's title and author as well as your name, email address, and phone number. I will carefully review your comments and share them with the author and editors who worked on the book.

Email:    feedback@quepublishing.com

Mail:    Que Publishing
ATTN: Reader Feedback
800 East 96th Street
Indianapolis, IN 46240 USA

## READER SERVICES

Visit our website and register this book at informit.com/register for convenient access to any updates, downloads, or errata that might be available for this book.

# IT'S AS EASY AS 1-2-3

Each part of this book is made up of a series of short, instructional lessons, designed to help you understand basic information.

 Each step is fully illustrated to show you how it looks onscreen

 Each task includes a series of quick, easy steps designed to guide you through the procedure.

Items that you select or click in menus, dialog boxes, tabs, and windows are shown in **bold**.

Tips, notes, and cautions give you a heads-up for any extra information you may need while working through the task.

**How to Drag:** Point to the starting place or object. Hold down the mouse button (right or left per instructions), move the mouse to the new location, and then release the button.

**Click:** Click the left mouse button once.

**Click & Type:** Click once where indicated and begin typing to enter your text or data.

**Selection:** Highlights the area onscreen discussed in the step or task.

**Double-click:** Click the left mouse button twice in rapid succession.

**Right-click:** Click the right mouse button once.

**Pointer arrow:** Highlights an item on the screen you need to point to or focus on in the step or task.

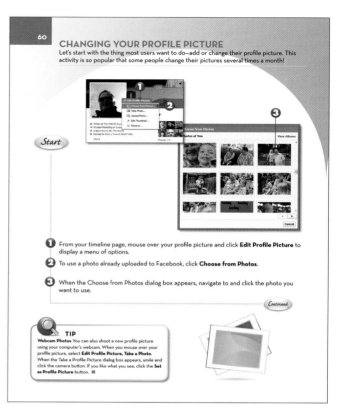

60

**CHANGING YOUR PROFILE PICTURE**

Let's start with the thing most users want to do—add or change their profile picture. This activity is so popular that some people change their pictures several times a month!

*Start*

1. From your timeline page, mouse over your profile picture and click **Edit Profile Picture** to display a menu of options.

2. To use a photo already uploaded to Facebook, click **Choose from Photos**.

3. When the Choose from Photos dialog box appears, navigate to and click the photo you want to use.

*Continued*

**TIP**

**Webcam Photos** You can also shoot a new profile picture using your computer's webcam. When you mouse over your profile picture, select **Edit Profile Picture, Take a Photo.** When the Take a Profile Picture dialog box appears, smile and click the camera button. If you like what you see, click the **Set as Profile Picture** button.

# INTRODUCTION TO EASY FACEBOOK

Facebook is the latest thing, a so-called social network that enables you to share the important things in your life with the people who are important to you. Although that seems like a good thing, it might also sound a little scary or difficult to some. Well, it doesn't need to be. In fact, using Facebook can be *easy*—if you know what to do.

That's where this book comes in. *Easy Facebook* is an illustrated, step-by-step guide to using Facebook to communicate with your friends and family. You'll learn how Facebook works, how to set up a new account, how to find out what your friends are up to, and how to let them know what you're doing, too. All you have to do is look at the pictures and follow the instructions. Pretty easy.

After you learn the basics, I'll show you how to do lots of fun and useful stuff on Facebook. You'll learn how to find new friends on Facebook and organize your friends into convenient lists; how to view friends' photos and videos, and how to share your own pictures and movies; how to personalize your Facebook timeline page and profile information; how to "like" celebrities and companies; how to use third-party apps and play social games; how to share events and celebrate birthdays; how to chat with friends via text or video; and how to use Facebook from your iPhone. We'll even cover important privacy issues, including what you should and shouldn't post to the Facebook site.

It's all rather easy. To help you find the information you need, I've organized *Easy Facebook* into 15 chapters.

Chapter 1, "How Facebook and Social Networking Work," takes you behind the scenes to learn all about the social networking phenomenon, and shows you how Facebook itself got started.

You'll also learn the basics of how the Facebook site works.

Chapter 2, "Getting Started with Facebook," shows you how to create a new Facebook account, then how to log in to and out of Facebook. You'll also learn how to navigate the Facebook site and use Facebook's convenient toolbar.

Chapter 3, "Finding and Visiting with Your Friends," helps you find new friends on the Facebook site and shows you how to invite them to join your friends list. You'll also learn how to view a friend's timeline page, block unwanted friends, and even "unfriend" someone you no longer want to hear from.

Chapter 4, "Reading Your News Feed and Ticker," shows you how to read all the status updates from your friends, in your Facebook news feed and ticker. You'll also learn how to comment on and like your friends' posts, how to hide posts from people and apps you don't like, and how to control the number of updates you see from any given individual.

Chapter 5, "Posting Status Updates," walks you through the process of keeping your friends informed of what you're up to. You'll learn how to post text-based status updates, as well as updates containing web links, photos, videos, and questions. You'll also learn how to tag your friends in posts and determine the privacy level of any given update—who, exactly, can view it.

Chapter 6, "Personalizing Your Timeline," shows you how to customize your Facebook presence. You'll learn how to change your profile picture, add a cover image, customize the top-of-page elements, hide and delete status updates, highlight your favorite updates, edit your activity log, add life events to your timeline, and update your profile information.

Chapter 7, "Organizing Your Friends into Lists," helps you group your friends into smaller lists that are easier to deal with. You'll also learn how to add and remove friends from your lists, how to post a status update to a list, and how to view status updates from only those people in a selected list.

Chapter 8, "Sharing Pictures," shows you how to view and comment on friends photos, and how to upload your own photos to Facebook. You'll learn how to download and print photos, how to comment and like photos, how to tag yourself and friends in your photos, and how to create and manage your own photo albums.

Chapter 9, "Sharing Videos," is all about viewing and uploading home movies and other videos. You'll learn how to view friends' videos, as well as upload your own video files, shoot videos with your webcam, and share on Facebook videos that you find on the YouTube site.

Chapter 10, "Text and Video Chatting," is all about communicating in real time with your Facebook friends. You'll learn how to open and participate in both text and video chats—the latter if you have a webcam on your PC, of course.

Chapter 11, "Working with Facebook Pages, Apps, and Games," shows you how to like your favorite celebrities, companies, and private figures on Facebook; how to install and use useful third-party applications; and how to play social games while you're using Facebook.

Chapter 12, "Sharing Events and Birthdays," shows you how to participate in others' Facebook events and how to create and invite others to your own events. You'll also learn how to celebrate your friends' birthdays on the Facebook site.

Chapter 13, "Keeping Private Things Private," is all about using Facebook smartly and safely. You'll learn what you should and shouldn't post on the Facebook site, and how to set Facebook's privacy levels—that is, how to determine who sees what you post online.

Chapter 14, "Managing Your Facebook Account," helps you find and manage all your Facebook account settings.

Chapter 15, "Using Facebook on the Go," is all about accessing Facebook from your iPhone. You'll learn how to read your news feed on your smartphone, and how to post status updates and photos from anywhere, anytime.

And that's not all. At the back of the book you'll find a glossary of common Facebook terms—so you can understand what everyone is talking about!

So, is using Facebook really this easy? You bet—just follow the simple step-by-step instructions, and you'll be social networking like a pro!

# HOW FACEBOOK AND SOCIAL NETWORKING WORK

Social networking enables people to share experiences and opinions with each other on community-based websites and on their mobile phones. It's a great way to keep up-to-date on what your friends and family are doing.

Each member of the social network posts his or her own personal profile on the community website. You use the information in these profiles to connect with other people you know on the network or with those who share your interests.

The goal is to create a network of these online "friends" and then share your activities with them via a series of message posts. All your online friends read your posts, as well as posts from other friends, in a continuously updated news feed. The news feed is the one place where you can read updates from all your online friends and family; it's where you find out what's really happening.

The biggest social network today is a site called Facebook; chances are many of your friends and family are already using it. Other popular social networks include Twitter, LinkedIn, Pinterest, and Google+.

# TOP SOCIAL MEDIA

Facebook

Twitter

LinkedIn

Pinterest

Google+

# UNDERSTANDING SOCIAL NETWORKING

A *social network* is a large website that hosts a community of users and makes it easy for those users to communicate with one another. Social networks enable users to share experiences and opinions with one another via short text messages—called *status updates*—or photos that are posted for public viewing by all of that person's friends on the site.

*Start*

1️⃣ Assemble your own personal network of online friends from other members of the social network.

2️⃣ When you post a new message, it's automatically distributed to everyone on your friends list.

*Continued*

**NOTE**

**Twitter** This (www.twitter.com) is different from other social networks in that it doesn't offer a lot of community features. What you get is a series of short (140 characters or less) text messages, called *tweets*, to keep you up-to-date on the activities of friends and celebrities. ■

**NOTE**

**LinkedIn** This (www.linkedin.com) is a social network for business professionals. It's great for business networking, keeping in touch with members of your profession, and job hunting. ■

**3** You can view all your friends' status updates on a single, continuously updated page.

**4** Social networks also let you share photos, videos, and links to other web pages with your online friends.

*End*

**NOTE**

**Pinterest** Pinterest (www.pinterest.com) is a new visual social network with broad appeal to women and nontechnical users. You "pin" interesting images to your online pinboards and then share your pins with your friends—who can "repin" the ones they particularly like. ■

**NOTE**

**Google+** Google+ (www.google.com/plus/) is a social network tied into Google's search engine and network of sites. It works much like Facebook, with posts collected in an online *stream* for easy reading. ■

# HOW FACEBOOK GOT STARTED

Facebook is the brainchild of Mark Zuckerberg, who came up with the concept while a student at Harvard. Facebook (originally called thefacebook) was originally intended as a site where college students could socialize online. Sensing opportunity beyond the college market, Facebook opened its site to high school students in 2005, and to all users over age 13 in 2006. Today, Facebook boasts more than 900 million members worldwide.

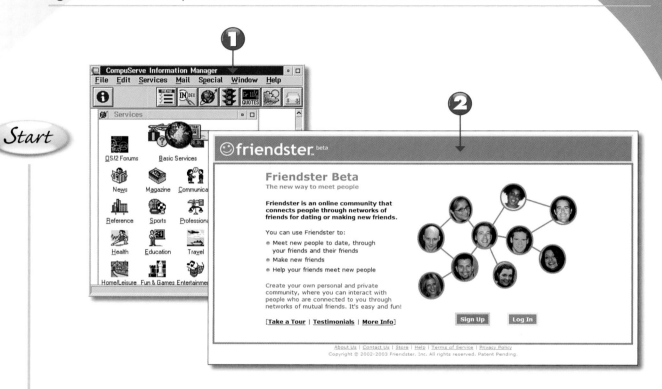

*Start*

**1** Today's social networks evolved from the earliest dial-up computer networks and bulletin board systems, such as CompuServe.

**2** The first fully formed social network was Friendster, which launched in 2002.

*Continued*

---

**NOTE**

**Proto-Social Networks** The early proto-social networks of the 1970s and 1980s, such as CompuServe, Prodigy, and TheWELL, predated the formal Internet and relied on dial-up computer connections. They offered topic-based discussion forums and chat rooms, but little else in the way of true social networking. ■

**NOTE**

**The Social Network** The story of Facebook's founding was told in the 2010 film *The Social Network*. Although some elements of the film are clearly fictitious, the movie is actually a fairly accurate retelling of events. ■

**3** Facebook launched in 2004 as thefacebook and became the most popular social networking site in 2008.

**4** Today, Facebook offers a variety of community-oriented features and is one of the most-visited sites on the entire Internet.

*End*

**NOTE**

**Facebook Goes Public** Facebook was a private company until May 2012, when it issued stock and went public. The company's initial public offering (IPO) was marred by errors, however, and the stock quickly dropped from its $38 opening share price. Still, the IPO valued the company at more than $100 billion—and made company founder Mark Zuckerberg an instant multibillionaire. ■

**NOTE**

**Other Social Media** Social networks aren't the only form of social media on the Internet. *Social bookmarking services*, such as Delicious and Reddit, let users share their favorite web pages with friends and colleagues online. *Blogs* are shared journals consisting of entries from the site's owner or creator. And *micro-blogging services*, such as Twitter, exist solely to broadcast short text posts from users to groups of followers. ■

# HOW FACEBOOK WORKS

Different people use Facebook for different reasons. Some people use Facebook to share important life events with friends and family. Others use Facebook to keep in constant touch with friends and acquaintances. Still others use Facebook to reconnect with old friends and colleagues from years past. In addition, many businesses use Facebook to forge close relationships with their most loyal customers.

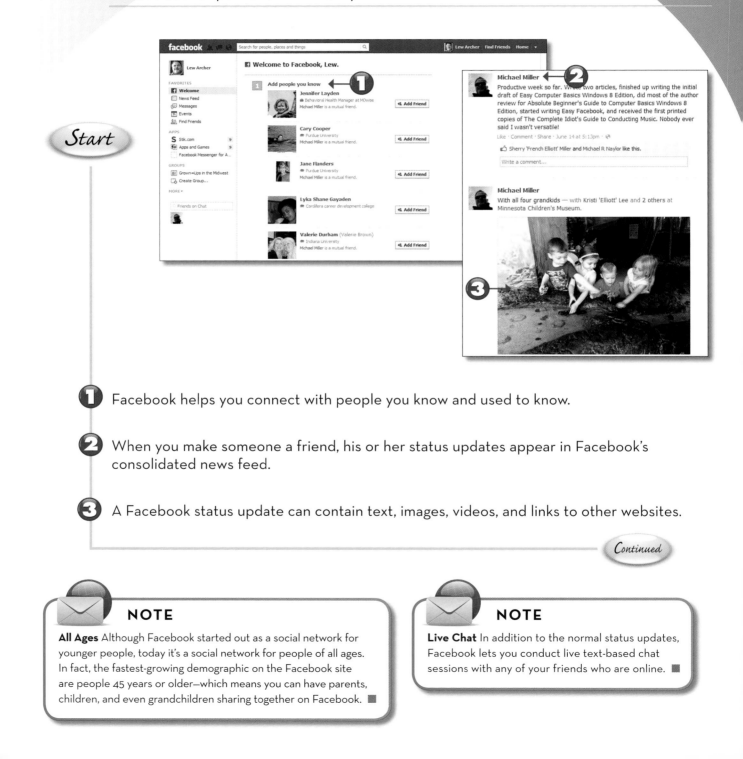

Start

1. Facebook helps you connect with people you know and used to know.

2. When you make someone a friend, his or her status updates appear in Facebook's consolidated news feed.

3. A Facebook status update can contain text, images, videos, and links to other websites.

Continued

**NOTE**

**All Ages** Although Facebook started out as a social network for younger people, today it's a social network for people of all ages. In fact, the fastest-growing demographic on the Facebook site are people 45 years or older—which means you can have parents, children, and even grandchildren sharing together on Facebook. ■

**NOTE**

**Live Chat** In addition to the normal status updates, Facebook lets you conduct live text-based chat sessions with any of your friends who are online. ■

**4** All your personal information and past status updates are consolidated on your personal *timeline*.

**5** Facebook also lets you schedule events you can share with your friends—and lets you respond to your friends' event requests

*End*

**NOTE**

**Apps and Games** Facebook also offers a variety of useful apps and fun games to play online. ■

**NOTE**

**Facebook Privacy** Facebook lets you determine who can see all your posts by default, or individual posts as you make them. You can make your content public for everyone to see, visible only to people on your friends list, or visible to (or hidden from) only selected individuals. ■

# GETTING STARTED WITH FACEBOOK

To use Facebook, you have to sign up for your own personal account. Your account is free; there's no fee to join and no monthly membership fees. (Facebook is almost entirely ad supported—which means you see ads on your home page.)

When you sign up for Facebook, you're prompted to enter a variety of personal information. The more Facebook knows about you, the more it can suggest friends and activities for to enjoy.

You're also prompted to find friends who are already using the Facebook site. This is how you start building your friends list—by finding people you know who are currently Facebook users.

# FACEBOOK'S HOME PAGE

Narrow display

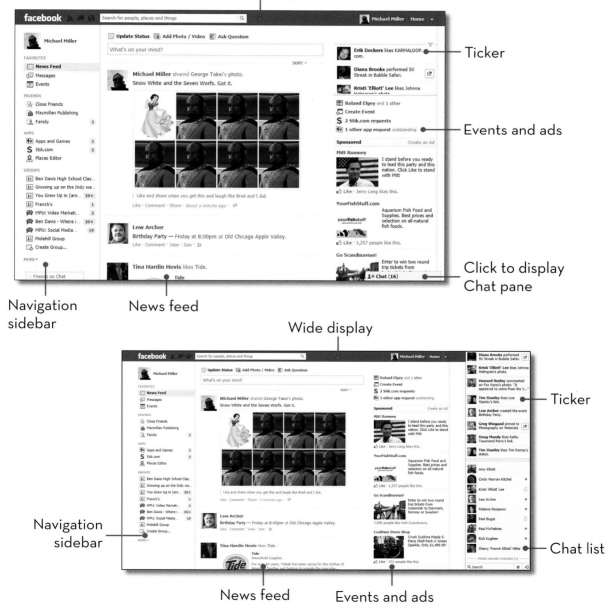

Ticker

Events and ads

Click to display
Chat pane

Navigation
sidebar

News feed

Wide display

Navigation
sidebar

Ticker

Chat list

News feed

Events and ads

# CREATING A NEW FACEBOOK ACCOUNT

To use Facebook, you have to sign up for an account and enter some personal information. Fortunately, signing up for an account is both easy and free.

**Start**

**Sign Up**
It's free and always will be.

First Name:
Last Name:
Your Email:
Re-enter Email:
New Password:
I am: Select Sex:
Birthday: Month: Day: Year:
Why do I need to provide my birthday?

By clicking Sign Up, you agree to our Terms and that you have read and understand our Data Use Policy, including our Cookie Use.

**Sign Up**

**1** Use your web browser to go to Facebook's home page at www.facebook.com.

**2** Go to the Sign Up section and enter your first and last name into the First Name and Last Name boxes.

**3** Enter your email address into the Your Email box and then re-enter into the Re-enter Email box.

**4** Enter your desired password into the New Password box. Your password should be at least six characters in length.

Continued

**NOTE**

**Email Sign In** You use your email address to sign into Facebook each time you enter the site. ■

**TIP**

**Password Security** To make your password more secure (harder for someone else to guess), include a mix of alphabetic, numeric, and special characters, such as punctuation marks. Longer passwords are also more secure. ■

**Sign Up**
It's free and always will be.

First Name: Samuel

Last Name: Spade

Your Email: samspade@archer.net

Re-enter Email: samspade@archer.net

New Password: •••••••

I am: Select Sex: ▾ **5**

Birthday: Month: ▾ Day: ▾ Year: ▾ **6**
Why do I need to provide my birthday?

By clicking Sign Up, you agree to our Terms and that you have read and understand our Data Use Policy, including our Cookie Use.

 Sign Up

**7**

**5** Pull down the I Am list and select your gender.

**6** Select your date of birth from the Birthday lists.

**7** Click the **Sign Up** button.

*End*

## NOTE

**CAPTCHA** When Facebook displays the Security Check page, you're prompted to enter the "secret words" from the CAPTCHA into the Text in the Box box. A CAPTCHA is a type of challenge-response test to ensure that you're actually a human being, rather than a computer program. Websites use CAPTCHAs to cut down on the amount of computer-generated spam they receive. ■

## NOTE

**Email Confirmation and More** After you click the final **Sign Up** button, Facebook sends you an email message asking you to confirm your new Facebook account; when you receive this email, click the link to proceed. You'll then be prompted to find friends who are already on Facebook and to fill in a few personal details for your profile page. You can perform these tasks now or at a later time, as we'll discuss later in this book. ■

# LOGGING IN TO FACEBOOK

You use your email address—and the password you created during the signup process—to log in to your Facebook account. Once you're logged in, Facebook displays your home page.

**Start**

**1** Use your web browser to go to www.facebook.com.

**2** Enter your email address into the Email or Phone box.

**3** Enter your password into the Password box.

**4** Click the **Log In** button.

**End**

**TIP**

**Phone Login** If you've entered your phone number into your personal Facebook profile, you can also log in to Facebook using this number. This is convenient when you're accessing Facebook primarily via mobile phone. ■

**TIP**

**Stay Logged In** If you don't want to enter your email and password every time you access the Facebook site, check the **Keep Me Logged In** option when you're logging in. This will keep your Facebook session open even if you visit another website between Facebook pages. ■

# LOGGING OUT OF FACEBOOK

You probably want to log out of Facebook if you're not going to be active for an extended period of time. Once you've logged out, you need to log back in before you can again access your Facebook content.

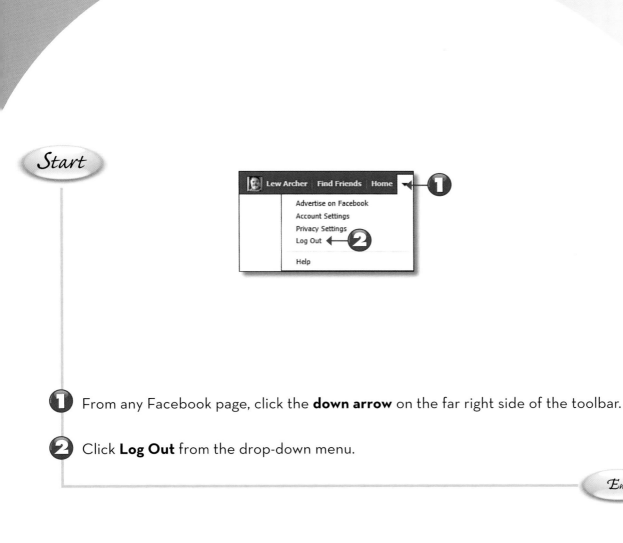

From any Facebook page, click the **down arrow** on the far right side of the toolbar.

Click **Log Out** from the drop-down menu.

**TIP**

**Switching Users** You also want to log out of your Facebook account if you want another user to log in using your computer. ■

# USING THE FACEBOOK TOOLBAR

The toolbar that appears at the top of every Facebook page is your primary means of navigating the Facebook site. The toolbar also provides notification when you have messages waiting or if a friend engages you in a specific activity.

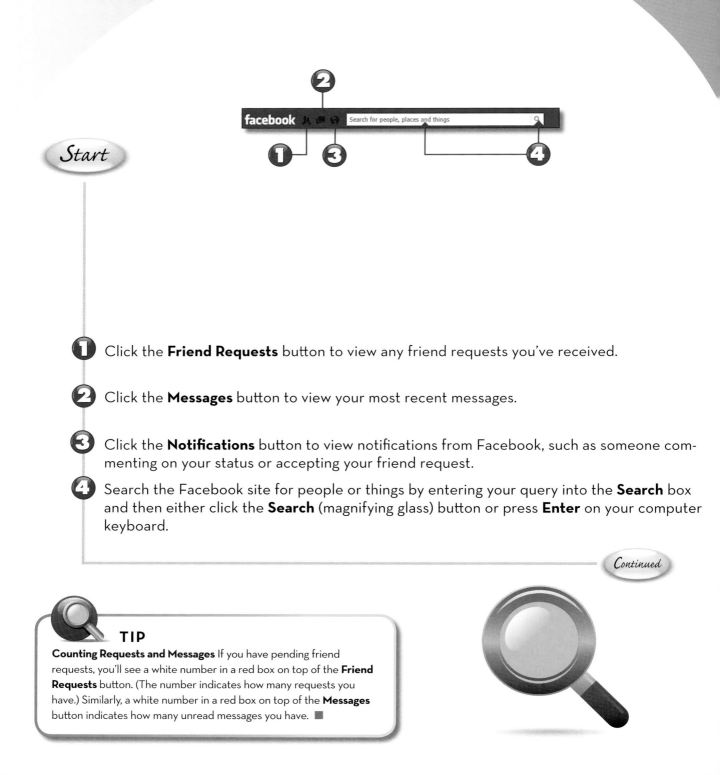

**Start**

**1** Click the **Friend Requests** button to view any friend requests you've received.

**2** Click the **Messages** button to view your most recent messages.

**3** Click the **Notifications** button to view notifications from Facebook, such as someone commenting on your status or accepting your friend request.

**4** Search the Facebook site for people or things by entering your query into the **Search** box and then either click the **Search** (magnifying glass) button or press **Enter** on your computer keyboard.

Continued

## TIP
**Counting Requests and Messages** If you have pending friend requests, you'll see a white number in a red box on top of the **Friend Requests** button. (The number indicates how many requests you have.) Similarly, a white number in a red box on top of the **Messages** button indicates how many unread messages you have. ■

**5** Visit your personal timeline page by clicking your name or picture.

**6** Click the **Find Friends** button (displayed on newer accounts only) to add new people to your Facebook friends list.

**7** Click the **Home** button to return to your Facebook home page.

**8** To access all sorts of account settings, including important privacy settings, click the **down arrow** on the far right side of the toolbar and make a selection from the drop-down menu.

*End*

**TIP**

**Two Ways to Go Home** You can go to your Facebook home page by clicking the **Home** button or the Facebook logo on the toolbar. ▪

**NOTE**

**Account Options** The options on the drop-down menu at the far right of the toolbar include Help, Account Settings, Privacy Settings, and Log Out. ▪

# NAVIGATING THE FACEBOOK SITE

Once you sign into your account, you see Facebook's Home page. You use the left column to click to various content on the site. The large column in the middle displays your *news feed*, a stream of posts from all your Facebook friends. The next column displays various Facebook ads and messages. The far-right column (visible on widescreen displays) hosts the *ticker* (a scrolling list of your friends' activity) and the Chat panel, for messaging online friends in real time.

1. Sign in to your Facebook account and select **News Feed** in the Favorites section of the navigation sidebar.

2. View status updates from your friends in the news feed.

3. View real-time activity in the ticker.

4. Post new status updates from the box at the top of the page.

*Continued*

## TIP

**Three or Four Columns** Facebook displays four columns on certain widescreen displays, but only three columns on smaller displays or when in a narrow desktop browser window. The three-column display combines the ticker, Chat panel, and notifications/ads into a single column on the right. ■

## TIP

**Sorting the News Feed** By default, the first items in the news feed are your Top Stories, those updates that Facebook "thinks" you should be most interested in. Other updates (what Facebook calls Recent Stories) are just below the Top Stories section; scroll down to view them. ■

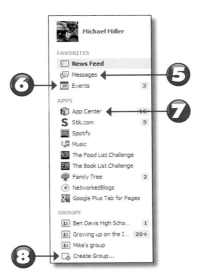

**5** To view messages in your Facebook inbox or send a private message to another user, click **Messages** in the Favorites section.

**6** To view pending events or schedule a new event, click **Events** in the Favorites section.

**7** To access any app you've enabled, click that app in the Apps section or click **App center** to view all available apps.

**8** To access any group you've joined, click that group in the Groups section or click **Create Group** to create your own topic-focused group.

*End*

**NOTE**

**Facebook Apps** A Facebook app is a third-party utility or service that provides specific usefulness to your Facebook experience. Some apps are actually games you can play online. ■

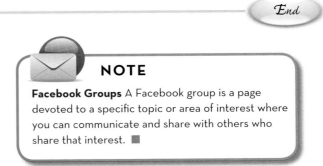

**NOTE**

**Facebook Groups** A Facebook group is a page devoted to a specific topic or area of interest where you can communicate and share with others who share that interest. ■

# Chapter 3

# FINDING AND VISITING WITH YOUR FRIENDS

Social networking is all about keeping in touch with friends. To get the most out of Facebook, then, you need to find some friends.

Because it's in Facebook's best interests for you to have as many connections as possible, the site makes it easy for you to find potential friends. Facebook suggests friends based on your personal history (where you've lived, worked, or gone to school), mutual friends (friends of people you're already friends with), and Facebook users who are in your email contacts lists. You can then invite any of these people to be your friends; if they accept, they're added to your Facebook friends list.

# VIEWING YOUR FRIENDS LIST

Click to make
friends list public
or private

Click to find new
friends

Click to view
a friend's
timeline

Search within
your friends
list

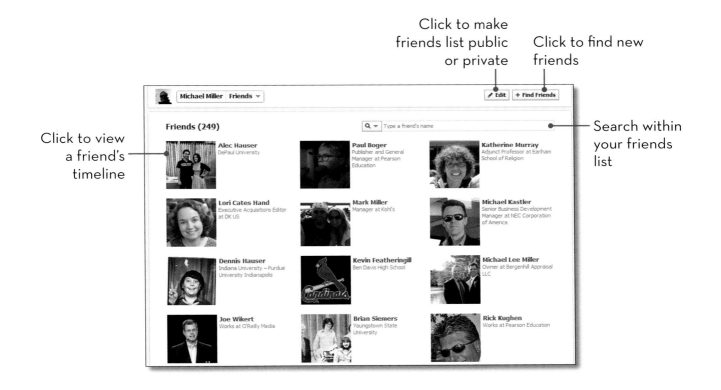

# FINDING NEW FRIENDS

The easiest way to find friends on Facebook is to let Facebook find them for you—based on the information you provided for your personal profile. The more Facebook knows about you, especially in terms of where you've worked and gone to school, the more friends it can find.

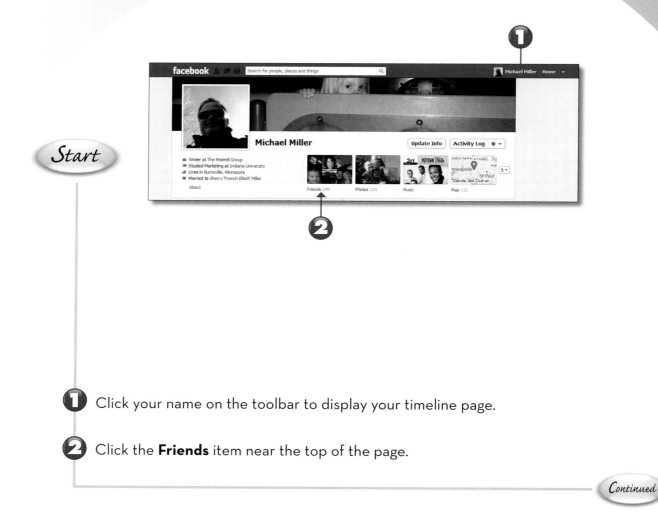

**Start**

**1** Click your name on the toolbar to display your timeline page.

**2** Click the **Friends** item near the top of the page.

Continued

**NOTE**

**News Feed** To see a person's status updates in your news feed, he must be on your friends list. ■

**NOTE**

**Suggested Friends** The people Facebook suggests as friends are typically people who went to the same schools you did, worked at the same companies you did, or are friends of your current friends. ■

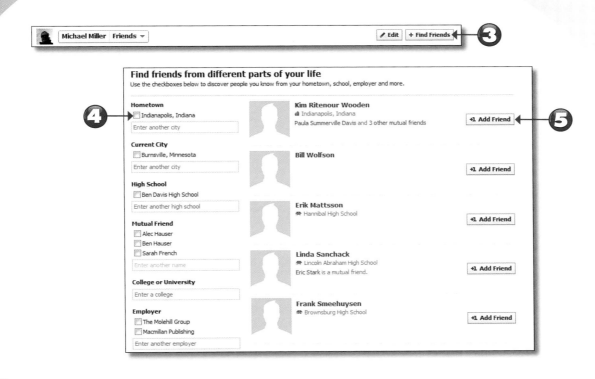

**3** When your Friends page appears, click the **Find Friends** button.

**4** The next page displays a list of people that Facebook thinks might be friends. You can filter this list by various criteria by checking the appropriate options in the left hand column.

**5** To invite any individual to be your friend, click the **Add Friend** button.

*End*

### NOTE

**Invitations** Facebook doesn't automatically add a person to your friends list. Instead, that person receives an invitation to be your friend; she can accept or reject the invitation. ■

### TIP

**Filtering Friends** Facebook lets you filter the list of potential friends by Hometown, Current City, High School, Mutual Friend(s), College or University, Employer, or Graduate School (if you so attended). For example, to search for folks who you went to high school with, check the appropriate **High School** box. ■

# FINDING FRIENDS VIA EMAIL

Another way to find Facebook friends is to let Facebook look through your email contact lists for people who are also Facebook members. You can then invite those people to be your friends.

**Start**

**1** Click the **Friend Requests** button on the Facebook toolbar.

**2** Select the **Find Friends** link in the drop-down menu.

**3** When the Friends Step 1 page appears, select the email service you use.

**4** If you use a web-based email service, such as Hotmail or Gmail, enter your email address and click the **Find Friends** button. (If prompted, enter your email password, too.)

*Continued*

## NOTE

**Email Friends** This process works by matching the email addresses in your contact lists with the email addresses users provide as their Facebook logins. When Facebook finds a match, it suggests that person as a potential friend. ■

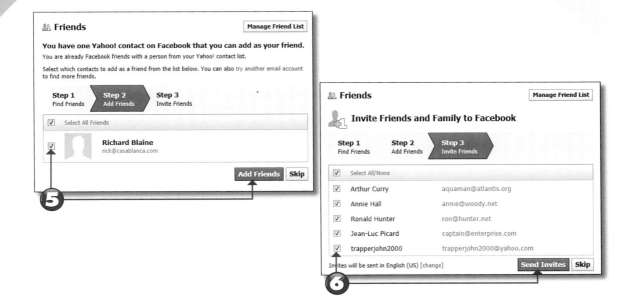

**5** Facebook now displays a list of your email contacts who are also Facebook members. Check the box next to each person with whom you'd like to be friends and click the **Add Friends** button to send friend requests to these contacts.

**6** You now see a list of your other friends who are not yet Facebook members. Check the box next to each person you'd like to become a Facebook member (and join your friends list) and click the **Send Invites** button.

*Continued*

---

### NOTE

**Accept or Decline** When Facebook sends friend requests to the people you selected, the person can accept or decline the request. If a person accepts your request, you become friends with that person. If a person does not accept your request, you don't become friends. (Nor are you notified if your friend request is declined.) ■

### NOTE

**Contact Searching** Facebook can search contacts from a variety of web-based email and communications services, including AOL (mail and messenger), Comcast, Gmail, sbcglobal.net, Skype, Verizon.net, Windows Live Hotmail, and Windows Live Messenger. ■

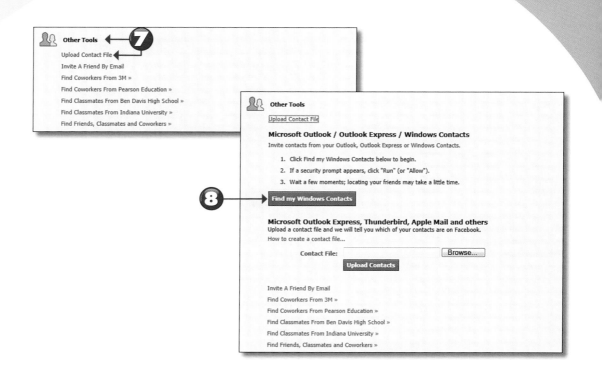

**7** If you use Microsoft Outlook, Outlook Express, or Windows contacts program to check your email or manage your contacts, scroll down the page and click **Other Tools** and then select **Upload Contact File**.

**8** When the page changes, click the **Find My Windows Contacts** button and follow the onscreen instructions to proceed.

*Continued*

**NOTE**

**Microsoft Outlook** Microsoft Outlook is the email component in the Microsoft Office suite. It is a popular email client in the corporate environment. ■

**NOTE**

**Outlook Express** Microsoft Outlook Express is Microsoft's less full-featured email client. It is no longer distributed under its original name; it's now called Windows Live Mail (or, in Windows 8, simply Mail). ■

**9** If you use another software program to manage your email, scroll down the page and click **Other Tools** and then select **Upload Contact File**.

**10** When the page changes, click the **Browse** or **Choose File** button and then navigate to and select your email contacts file.

**11** When you return to the Friends page, click the **Upload Contacts** button to upload your email contacts list to Facebook and display a list of email contacts who are also Facebook members.

*End*

### NOTE

**Other Email Programs** Other popular email clients include Mozilla Thunderbird, Eudora, and Apple Mail. All of these programs store their contacts in a separate file that can be uploaded to Facebook for matching. ■

# ACCEPTING A FRIEND REQUEST

Facebook will notify you via email when someone has requested to be your friend. You can also access all pending friend requests from the Facebook toolbar.

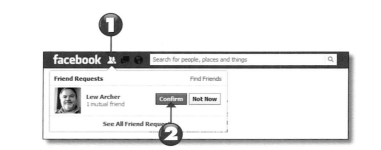

*Start*

**1** Click the **Friend Request** button on the Facebook toolbar.

**2** All pending friend requests are displayed in the pull-down menu. Click **Confirm** to accept a specific friend request and be added to that person's friends list.

*End*

**TIP**

**Accept or Decline** You do not have to accept all friend requests. If you receive a request from someone you don't know (or someone you don't like), click the **Not Now** button and continue to ignore that person on Facebook. ▪

**TIP**

**View All Friend Requests** If you have more than a handful of pending friend requests, they all can't be shown in the drop-down menu. Click **See All Friend Requests** to view a complete list of pending friend requests. ▪

# BLOCKING UNWANTED USERS

If you think that someone is stalking you on Facebook, you can completely block all contact from that person by adding this individual to what Facebook calls your *block list*. People on your block list cannot view your timeline page, send you private messages, or even find you in a search of the Facebook site. It's a great way to shield yourself from online stalkers—or just people you never want to hear from again.

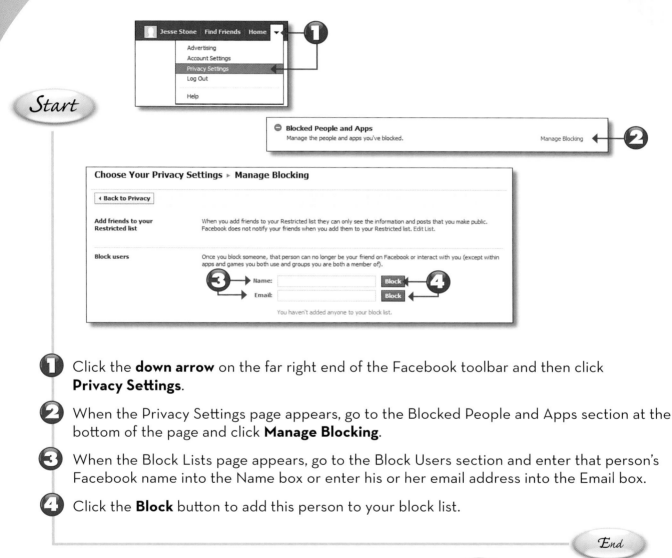

*Start*

Click the **down arrow** on the far right end of the Facebook toolbar and then click **Privacy Settings**.

When the Privacy Settings page appears, go to the Blocked People and Apps section at the bottom of the page and click **Manage Blocking**.

When the Block Lists page appears, go to the Block Users section and enter that person's Facebook name into the Name box or enter his or her email address into the Email box.

Click the **Block** button to add this person to your block list.

*End*

### TIP

**Unblocking** People you've blocked are listed on the Block Lists page. To unblock a given individual, click the **Unblock** link next to his or her name. ■

# UNFRIENDING A FRIEND

What do you do about those friends who you really don't want to be friends with anymore? You can, at any time, remove any individual from your Facebook friends list. This is called *unfriending* the person, and it happens all the time.

**Start**

**1** Click your name on the Facebook toolbar to display your timeline page.

**2** Click the **Friends** graphic to display your Friends page.

**3** Click the name of the person you want to unfriend.

*Continued*

## NOTE

**No One's the Wiser** When you unfriend a person on Facebook, that person doesn't know that he's been unfriended. There are no official notices sent. ■

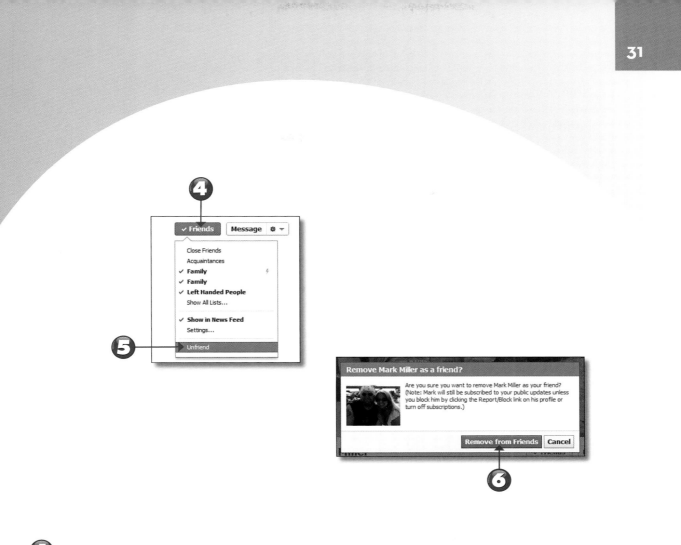

**4** When the person's timeline page appears, mouse over the **Friends** button to display the pop-up menu.

**5** Select **Unfriend**.

**6** When the Remove as a Friend? dialog box appears, click the **Remove from Friends** button.

*End*

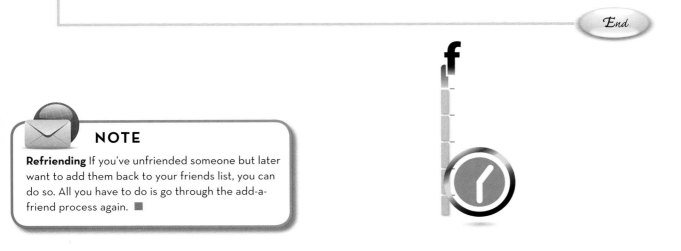

**NOTE**

**Refriending** If you've unfriended someone but later want to add them back to your friends list, you can do so. All you have to do is go through the add-a-friend process again. ■

# VIEWING A FRIEND'S TIMELINE

After you've added people to your Facebook friends list, you can easily check up on what they've been up to by visiting their timeline pages. A Facebook timeline is their profile on the Facebook site; it displays not only their personal information, but also all the status updates they've made, on a chronological timeline.

1. To display a person's timeline page, click that person's name anywhere on the Facebook site.

2. Click the **About** link to view additional personal information.

3. Click the **Friends** link to view all of this person's Facebook friends.

4. Click the **Photos** link to view the photographs this person has uploaded to Facebook.

Continued

## TIP

**Hide Status Updates** By default, status updates from your friends will appear in your Facebook news feed. To remove this person's posts from your news feed, while still keeping her as a friend, click the **Friends** button and uncheck the **Show in News Feed** option. ■

## NOTE

**Other Elements** Because everyone can customize his or her timeline page, the elements displayed at the top of the page will vary from person to person. Popular elements (in addition to Friends and Photos) include Map (a map of that person's location), Likes, Notes, Subscribers, and Subscriptions. To view those elements not automatically displayed, click the down arrow at the far end of the elements row. ■

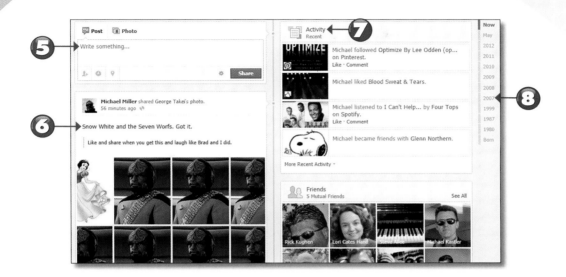

**5** Post a message to this person.

**6** Read individual status updates; scroll down to view older updates.

**7** View this person's recent Facebook activity.

**8** Click the timeline to view activity from a selected time period.

*End*

**NOTE**

**Timeline Order** Status updates and other activities are placed on the timeline in the month they occurred, but not necessarily in order within that month. Facebook attempts to place more important items first within a given month. ■

**NOTE**

**Timeline Length** Facebook will place all activities it knows about on an individual's timeline. Because it knows everyone's date of birth (entered when a person first joins Facebook), that is typically the earliest date on the timeline. Unless an individual enters dates for other events (such as graduations, marriage, vacations, and the like), the next item on the timeline will be a person's first Facebook post. ■

## Chapter 4

# READING YOUR NEWS FEED AND TICKER

When you sign into Facebook and open your home page, you see something called the *news feed*. As the name implies, this is a feed of the most recent status updates ("news") from people on your friends list.

Most updates are short text messages, although updates can also include photos, videos, notices of upcoming events, and links to other web pages. If there's a photo in a status update, click the photo to view it at a larger size. If there's a video in the status update, click the video to begin playback. If an event is listed in the status update, click it to read more details and RSVP, if you're invited. If there's a link in the status update, click it to leave Facebook and visit the linked-to page. It's pretty easy to figure out.

# ELEMENTS OF A STATUS UPDATE

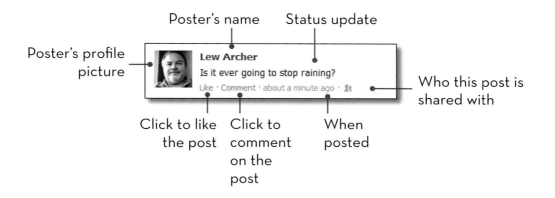

Poster's name

Status update

Poster's profile picture

Who this post is shared with

Click to like the post

Click to comment on the post

When posted

# VIEWING THE NEWS FEED

The status updates in your Facebook news feed are displayed more or less in reverse chronological order. This means that the most recent updates are at the top and the older ones are at the bottom—with the notable exception that Top Stories appear before Recent Stories. To view even older updates, scroll to the bottom of the page and click the **Older Posts** button.

*Start*

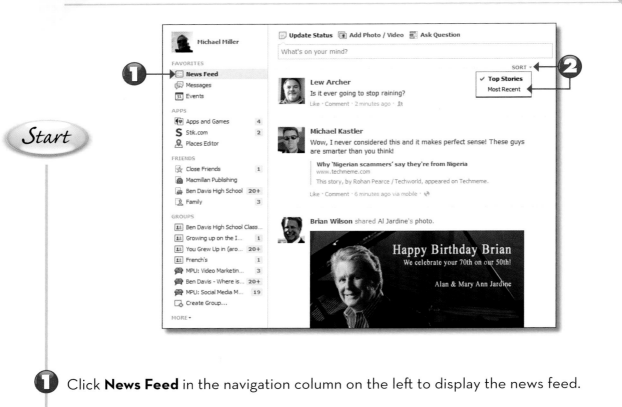

**1** Click **News Feed** in the navigation column on the left to display the news feed.

**2** By default, Facebook displays your Top Stories first. To instead display the Most Recent stories first, click the **Sort** link at the top of the news feed and select **Most Recent** from the pop-up menu.

*Continued*

---

**NOTE**

**Top Stories and Recent Stories** Facebook divides the news feed into Top Stories and Recent Stories. Top Stories are those updates that Facebook thinks are most important; Recent Stories are everything else. ■

**NOTE**

**Posting Rules—Not** Your friends are likely to post about what they're doing and what they're thinking. Some people post once a day, some post once a week, some post several times a day, and some don't post much at all. There are no rules or guidelines as to how often someone should post or what they should post about, so you never know what your friends will post. ■

**3** If the post contains a photograph, click the photo to display it in a larger viewing window (called the *lightbox*).

**4** Click the **X** (or press the **Esc** key on your keyboard) to close the lightbox and return to your news feed.

Continued

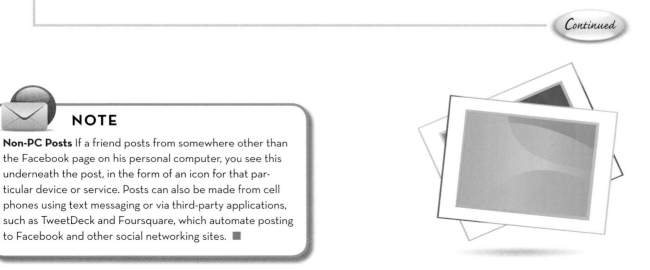

## NOTE

**Non-PC Posts** If a friend posts from somewhere other than the Facebook page on his personal computer, you see this underneath the post, in the form of an icon for that particular device or service. Posts can also be made from cell phones using text messaging or via third-party applications, such as TweetDeck and Foursquare, which automate posting to Facebook and other social networking sites. ■

**5** If the post contains a video, click the video thumbnail to begin playback within the news feed.

**6** If the post contains a link to another web page, click the link to open that page in a new tab in your web browser.

*End*

**NOTE**

**Web Page Images** Most web links in Facebook status updates are accompanied by an image from the linked-to web page. ■

# VIEWING THE TICKER

The news feed isn't the only place to find new information from your friends. At the top of the right column is something called the *ticker*, which is a scrolling list of what your friends are doing, updated in real time. This list includes more than just status updates; it also includes comments your friends make on other updates, photos uploaded, songs listened to on Spotify and other music services, and more. Just about anything Facebook knows about, however unimportant, is scrolled here.

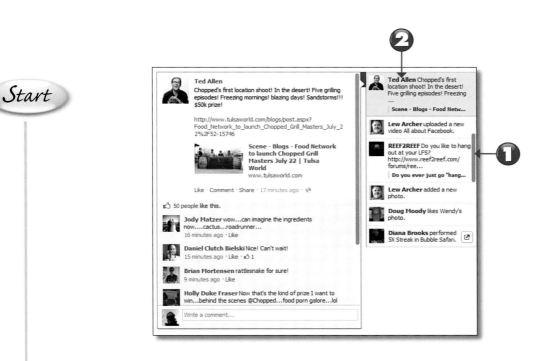

*Start*

1. To view older posts, mouse over the ticker to display the scrollbar, and then drag the scrollbar down.

2. To display the full post, along with comments and likes, click the item in the ticker.

*End*

## NOTE

**Duplicative Activity** For many users, the ticker duplicates to a large degree what you see in the news feed. That said, the ticker will include activities, such as comments on other posts, that don't normally appear in the news feed. ■

# COMMENTING ON FRIENDS' POSTS

Sometimes you read a friend's post, and you want to respond to it. To this end, Facebook enables you to comment on just about any post your friends make. These comments then appear under the post in your news feed.

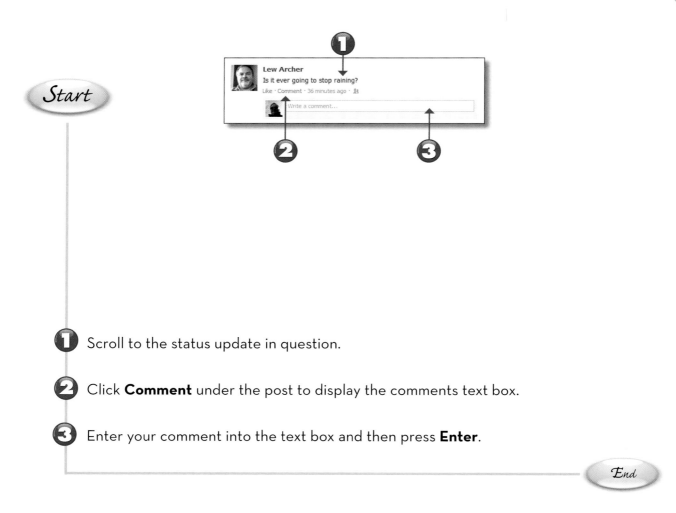

*Start*

**1** Scroll to the status update in question.

**2** Click **Comment** under the post to display the comments text box.

**3** Enter your comment into the text box and then press **Enter**.

*End*

**NOTE**

**Comments** When a post has comments, the number of comments made appears underneath the original post. ▪

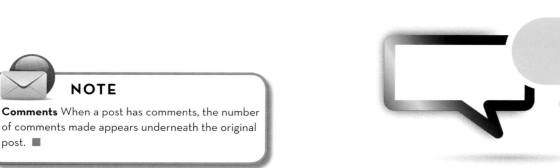

# LIKING A POST

You can also "like" a post without having to enter a comment about it. When you like a post, it puts a little thumbs-up icon under the post, along with a message that you "like this."

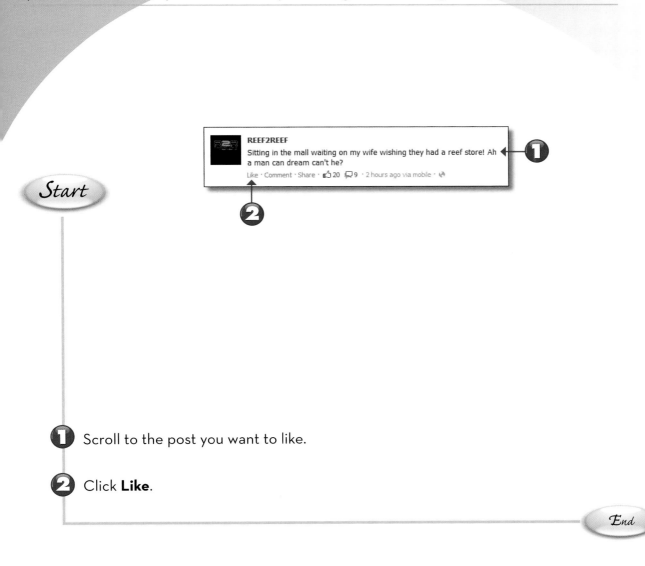

**Start**

**1** Scroll to the post you want to like.

**2** Click **Like**.

**End**

**NOTE**

**Like and Comment** You can both like and comment on a post; they're not mutually exclusive. ■

**TIP**

**Unliking a Post** If you later decide you don't like a given post, you can choose to "unlike" it. Just return to the post and click **Unlike**. ■

# HIDING POSTS FROM FRIENDS YOU DON'T LIKE

Over time, you will find that some of the people on your friends list, as well as some pages you subscribe to, serve up rather uninteresting posts. If you'd rather not read these posts, you can hide them from displaying in your news feed—without unfriending the person.

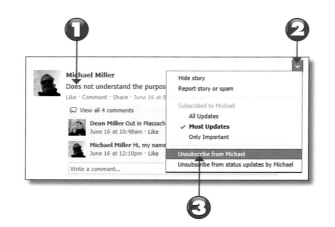

**Start**

① Navigate to and mouse over a post from a friend you want to hide; this displays a down arrow to the right of the post.

② Click the **down arrow** to display a menu of options.

③ Select **Unsubscribe from *Friend***. (Replace *Friend* with your friend's Facebook name.) This hides all future status updates from this person.

Continued

**TIP**

**Resubscribing** You can resubscribe to a friend's posts by opening that person's timeline page, clicking the **Friends** button, and selecting **Show in News Feed** from the pop-up menu. ■

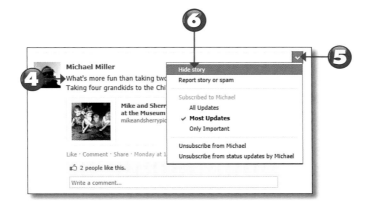

4 You can also hide individual status updates from your news feed. Mouse over the update you want to hide to display the down arrow.

5 Click the **down arrow**.

6 Select **Hide story**.

*End*

**CAUTION**

**Once It's Gone, It's Gone** When you hide a specific status update, you can't redisplay in your news feed. Once hidden, a post stays hidden. ■

# HIDING POSTS FROM APPS AND GAMES

Some status updates aren't really updates from a person, but rather updates from an application or game that the person is using or playing. These updates can be extremely annoying, especially when you see post after post from people who incessantly play Facebook's social games. Fortunately, you don't have to hide all the posts from your game-addicted friends; instead, you can choose to hide posts from the offending game or app.

Start

1 Navigate to and mouse over a post from the app or game you want to hide; this displays a down arrow to the right of the post.

2 Click the **down arrow**.

3 Click **Hide All by *Application***. (Replace *Application* with the app's name.) This hides all future status updates generated by this app or game.

End

## NOTE

**Annoying Updates** Examples of this type of app-generated post include status updates alerting you that a friend has achieved a certain level on Farmville, or killed someone in Mafia Wars, or read a new book in their Goodreads library. ■

## TIP

**Unblocking Blocked Apps** If you later want to display updates from an app you've previously blocked, click the **down arrow** on the right side of the Facebook toolbar and click **Privacy Settings**. When the Privacy Settings page appears, scroll to the Blocked People and Apps section and click **Manage Blocking**. On the Manage Blocking page, scroll to the Block Apps section and click **Unblock** for any app you want to redisplay in your news feed. ■

# DISPLAYING MORE OR FEWER UPDATES FROM A FRIEND

When you "friend" someone on Facebook, you essentially subscribe to his or her posts. There are three levels of subscription: You can view All Updates, Most Updates, or Only Important updates. The default level is Most Updates, but you can choose to view more or fewer updates if you want.

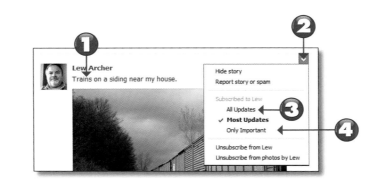

**Start**

1. Navigate to and mouse over one of this person's posts to display the down arrow.

2. Click the **down arrow**.

3. To view more updates from this person, select **All Updates** from the pop-up menu.

4. To view fewer updates from this person, select **Only Important** from the pop-up menu.

**End**

## TIP
**More Fine-Tuning** To further fine-tune the types of posts you see from a specific friend, go to that person's timeline page, click the **Friends** button, and then click **Settings**. You can then check or uncheck the types of posts you do or don't want to receive—Life Events, Status Updates, Photos, Games, Comments and Likes, Music and Videos, and Other Activity. ■

## Chapter 5

# POSTING STATUS UPDATES

On Facebook, you keep your friends and family up-to-date with your activities by posting regular *status updates*. Every status update you make is broadcast to everyone on your friends list, displayed in the news feeds on their home pages.

A status update is, at its most basic, a brief text message. It can be as short as a word or two, or it can be several paragraphs long; that's up to you. (Facebook lets you post updates with more than 60,000 characters, which should do for most folks.)

Although a basic status update is all text, you can also attach various multi-media elements to your status updates, including digital photographs, videos, questions, and links to other web pages. You can also "tag" other Facebook users and groups in your updates so that their names appear as clickable links (to their profile pages, of course).

# WHAT'S ON YOUR MIND?

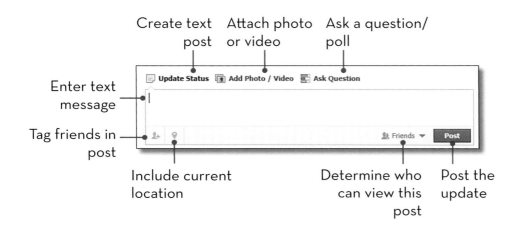

Create text post

Attach photo or video

Ask a question/ poll

Enter text message

Tag friends in post

Include current location

Determine who can view this post

Post the update

# POSTING A SIMPLE STATUS UPDATE

Facebook makes it easy to post a status update. You have to be signed in to your Facebook account; then it's a simple matter of opening your home page and creating the post.

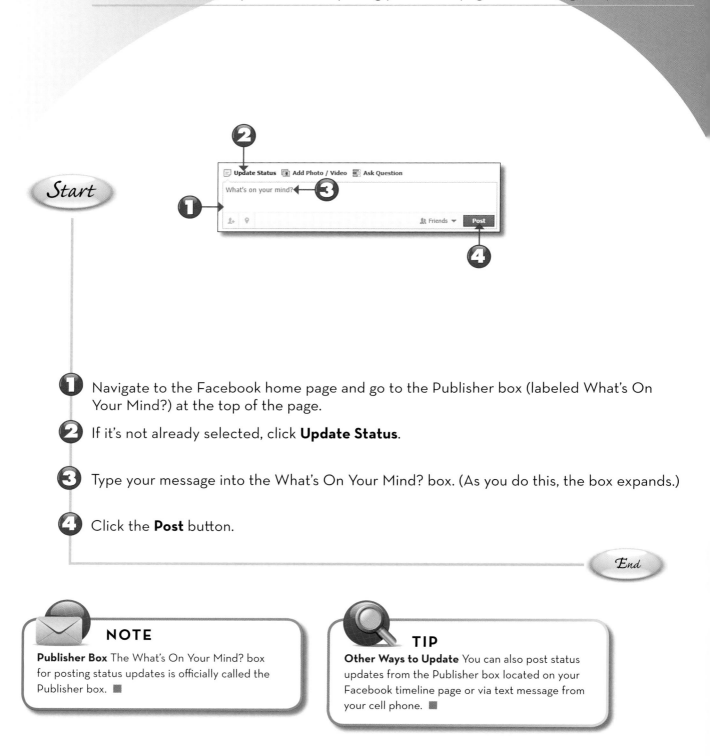

**Start**

**1** Navigate to the Facebook home page and go to the Publisher box (labeled What's On Your Mind?) at the top of the page.

**2** If it's not already selected, click **Update Status**.

**3** Type your message into the What's On Your Mind? box. (As you do this, the box expands.)

**4** Click the **Post** button.

**End**

### NOTE

**Publisher Box** The What's On Your Mind? box for posting status updates is officially called the Publisher box. ▪

### TIP

**Other Ways to Update** You can also post status updates from the Publisher box located on your Facebook timeline page or via text message from your cell phone. ▪

# POSTING A WEB LINK

You can include links to other web pages in your status updates. Not only does Facebook add a link to the specified page, it also lets you include a thumbnail image from that page with the status update.

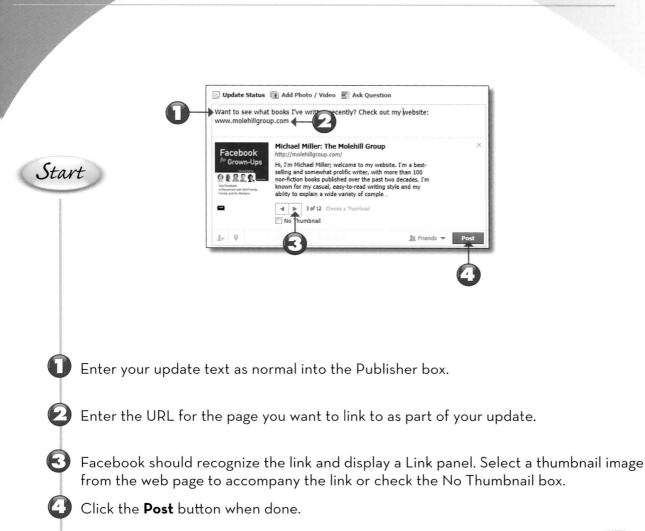

 Start

**1** Enter your update text as normal into the Publisher box.

**2** Enter the URL for the page you want to link to as part of your update.

**3** Facebook should recognize the link and display a Link panel. Select a thumbnail image from the web page to accompany the link or check the No Thumbnail box.

**4** Click the **Post** button when done.

End

---

### NOTE

**Facebook Grammar** Writing a Facebook status update is a bit like sending a text message on your cell phone. As such, status updates do not have to—and seldom do—conform to proper grammar, spelling, and sentence structure. It's common to abbreviate longer words, use familiar acronyms, substitute single letters and numbers for whole words, and refrain from all punctuation. ■

### TIP

**How Often Should You Post?** How often should you update your Facebook status? There's no good answer to that question. Some people post once a week, others post daily, others post several times a day. In general, you should post when you have something interesting to share—and not because you feel obligated to make a post. ■

# POSTING A PHOTO OR VIDEO

Facebook lets you embed digital photographs and videos in your posts. It's the Facebook equivalent of attaching a file to an email message.

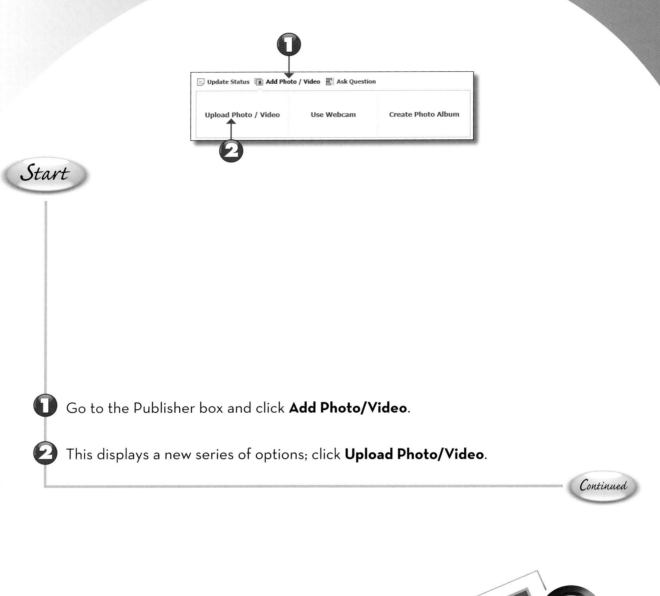

**Start**

**1** Go to the Publisher box and click **Add Photo/Video**.

**2** This displays a new series of options; click **Upload Photo/Video**.

*Continued*

**TIP**

**Webcam** You can also post pictures and videos taken with your computer's webcam. Just click **Use Webcam** instead of **Upload Photo/Video** and follow the onscreen instructions from there. ■

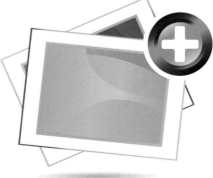

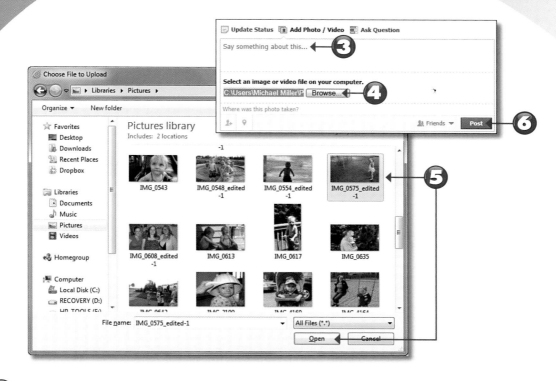

**3** Enter a short text message into the Say Something About This box.

**4** Click the **Browse** or **Choose File** button.

**5** When the Open dialog box appears, navigate to the photo or video file and click **Open**.

**6** Click the **Post** button when ready.

*End*

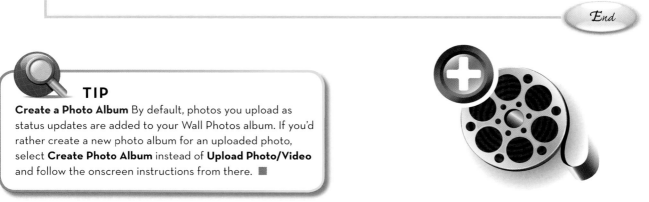

**TIP**

**Create a Photo Album** By default, photos you upload as status updates are added to your Wall Photos album. If you'd rather create a new photo album for an uploaded photo, select **Create Photo Album** instead of **Upload Photo/Video** and follow the onscreen instructions from there. ■

# POSTING A QUESTION

Facebook also lets you ask questions of the people on your friends list. You can use this to gather opinions, recommendations, and the like.

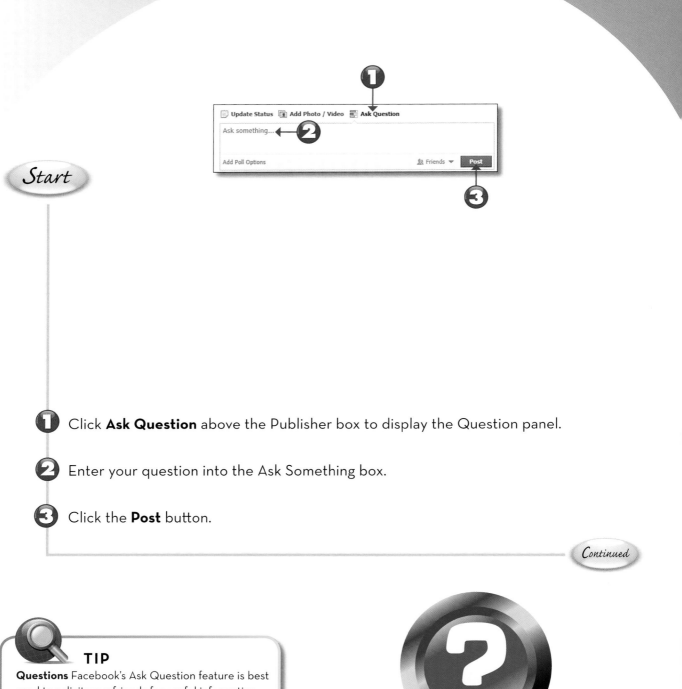

**Start**

1. Click **Ask Question** above the Publisher box to display the Question panel.

2. Enter your question into the Ask Something box.

3. Click the **Post** button.

Continued

### TIP

**Questions** Facebook's Ask Question feature is best used to solicit your friends for useful information, such as who knows a good plumber or how do you find a particular setting on a notebook computer. Don't expect a large number of answers. ■

4) When the question appears in your friends' news feeds, they can answer the question by filling in the blank and clicking the **Add** button.

5) The "live" answers to your question are shown on your own timeline page.

End

### CAUTION

**Qualifying Results** The results from any poll/question you ask on Facebook are decidedly unscientific. Because the question is only answered by friends who choose to do so, you can't rely on the results to represent a significant cross-section of the populace. ■

# ADDING YOUR LOCATION TO A POST

Facebook lets you identify your current location in any post you make. This lets you tell your friends where you are at any given time.

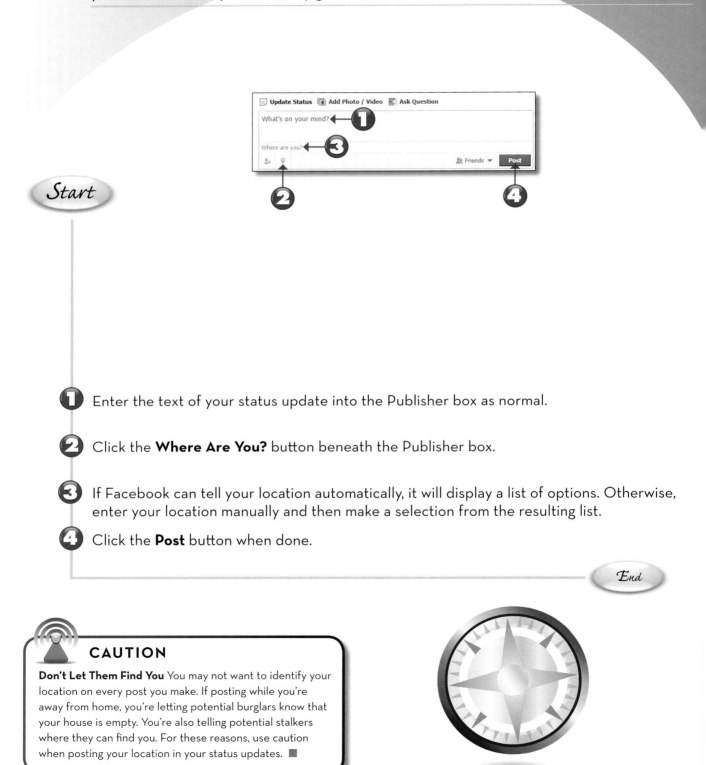

**Start**

**1** Enter the text of your status update into the Publisher box as normal.

**2** Click the **Where Are You?** button beneath the Publisher box.

**3** If Facebook can tell your location automatically, it will display a list of options. Otherwise, enter your location manually and then make a selection from the resulting list.

**4** Click the **Post** button when done.

**End**

### CAUTION

**Don't Let Them Find You** You may not want to identify your location on every post you make. If posting while you're away from home, you're letting potential burglars know that your house is empty. You're also telling potential stalkers where they can find you. For these reasons, use caution when posting your location in your status updates. ■

# TAGGING A FRIEND IN A POST

Sometimes you might want to mention one of your friends in a status update, or include a friend who was with you when the post was made. You can do this by "tagging" friends in your status updates; the resulting post includes a link to the tagged person or persons.

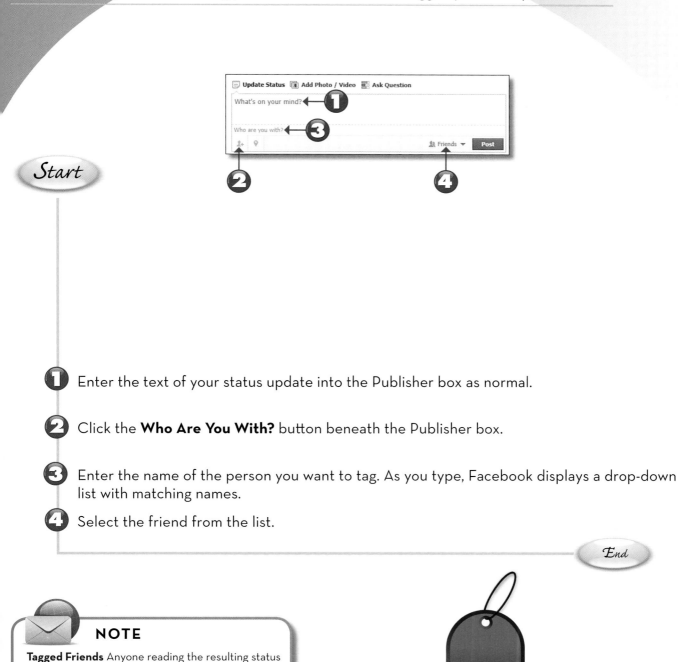

*Start*

1 Enter the text of your status update into the Publisher box as normal.

2 Click the **Who Are You With?** button beneath the Publisher box.

3 Enter the name of the person you want to tag. As you type, Facebook displays a drop-down list with matching names.

4 Select the friend from the list.

*End*

## NOTE

**Tagged Friends** Anyone reading the resulting status update sees the tagged person's name as a blue text link. Clicking the link displays the Facebook timeline page for the person tagged. ■

# DETERMINING WHO CAN VIEW A STATUS UPDATE

By default, everyone on Facebook can read every post you make. If you'd rather send a given post to a more select group of people, you can change the privacy settings for any individual post.

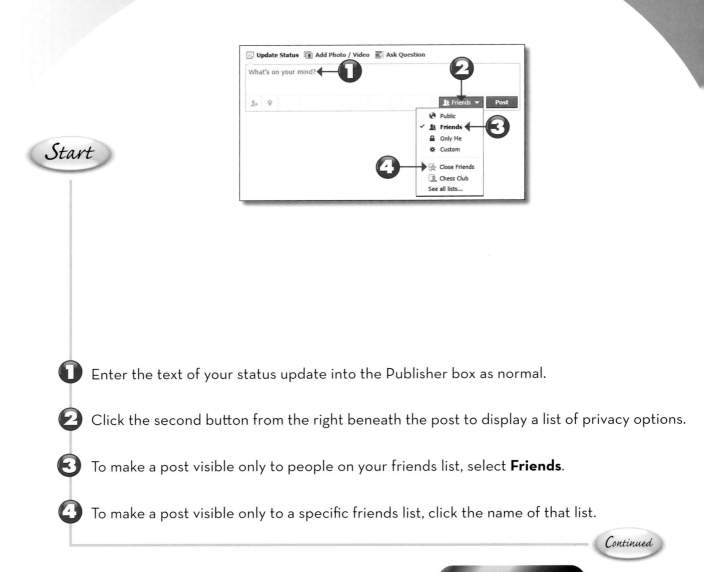

**Start**

**1** Enter the text of your status update into the Publisher box as normal.

**2** Click the second button from the right beneath the post to display a list of privacy options.

**3** To make a post visible only to people on your friends list, select **Friends**.

**4** To make a post visible only to a specific friends list, click the name of that list.

*Continued*

## CAUTION

**Keep Your Private Life Private** Think twice before making a post public. Many of the things you might post about are truly private and best not shared with the general public. Limit your more private posts to your friends only, or to specific people in your friends list. ■

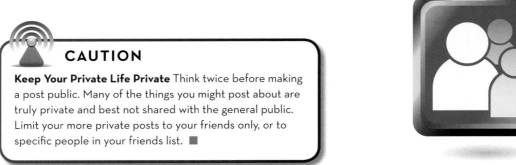

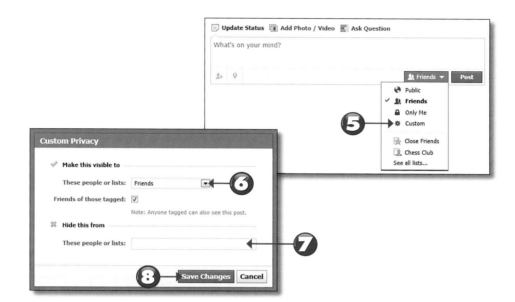

**5** To select specific individuals who can or can't view this post, click **Custom** to display the Custom Privacy box.

**6** To make this post visible to specific friends, friends lists, or networks, go to the Make This Visible To section and make a selection from the These People or Lists list.

**7** To hide this post from specific friends or friends lists, go to the Hide this From section and enter those names into the These People or Lists box.

**8** Click the **Save Changes** button when done.

*End*

**TIP**

**Friends of Tagged Friends** To let friends tagged in this post view the post, check the **Friends of Those Tagged** option. ■

## Chapter 6

# PERSONALIZING YOUR TIMELINE

All your personal information, including the status updates you've posted, are displayed on your Facebook timeline page. Your timeline is essentially your home base on Facebook, the place where all your Facebook friends can view all your information and activity.

You access your timeline page by clicking your name on the Facebook toolbar. At the very top of the page is a cover image, with your profile picture just below that and to the left. To the right of your picture is a set of informational boxes (Facebook calls them timeline apps) that link to your friends, photos, maps, and so forth.

That's the general information on your timeline page. Beneath that is the timeline itself, a listing of all your Facebook activity in reverse chronological order. Your timeline includes status updates, photo and video uploads, events, you name it. You can jump to any specific point on the timeline by clicking the literal timeline at the far right side of the page.

Most of what you see on your timeline page is set in stone by Facebook. That said, you can change your profile picture and cover image, edit or remove individual posts, and edit your profile information. It's all in the name of personalizing your timeline—if you so wish.

# EXAMINING THE TIMELINE

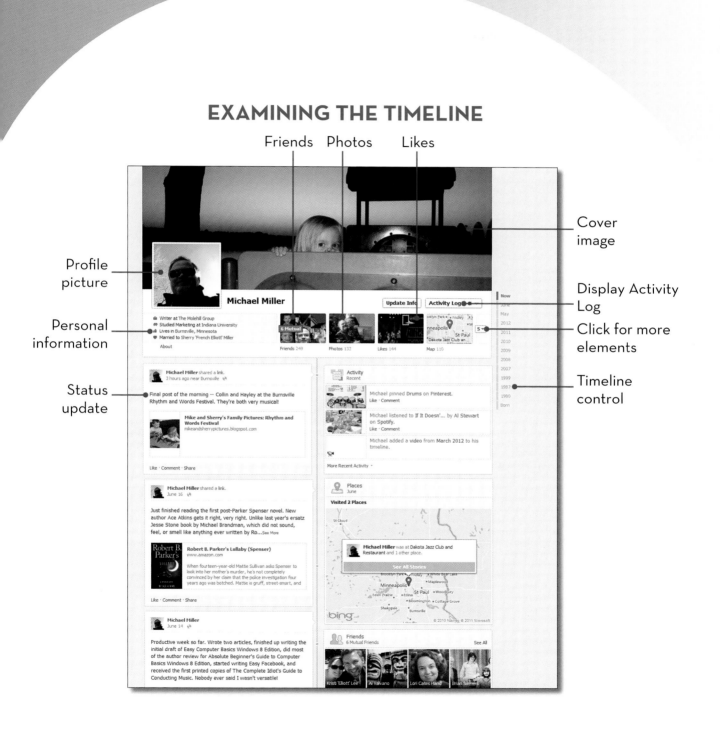

Friends  Photos  Likes

Cover image

Profile picture

Personal information

Status update

Display Activity Log

Click for more elements

Timeline control

# CHANGING YOUR PROFILE PICTURE

Let's start with the thing most users want to do—add or change their profile picture. This activity is so popular that some people change their pictures several times a month!

**Start**

1. From your timeline page, mouse over your profile picture and click **Edit Profile Picture** to display a menu of options.

2. To use a photo already uploaded to Facebook, click **Choose from Photos**.

3. When the Choose from Photos dialog box appears, navigate to and click the photo you want to use.

*Continued*

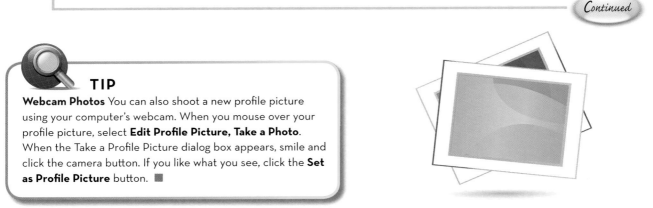

### TIP

**Webcam Photos** You can also shoot a new profile picture using your computer's webcam. When you mouse over your profile picture, select **Edit Profile Picture, Take a Photo**. When the Take a Profile Picture dialog box appears, smile and click the camera button. If you like what you see, click the **Set as Profile Picture** button. ∎

Drag the corners of the transparent box above to crop this photo into your profile picture. Done Cropping | Cancel

**4** Facebook now displays the chosen photo. Drag the highlight box over that portion of the photo you want to use for your profile.

**5** Click and drag any corner of the highlight box to crop the photo differently.

**6** Click **Done Cropping** when done. The photo, as cropped, now becomes your profile photo.

Continued

**TIP**

**Remove Your Picture** To remove the current profile picture without replacing it with a new picture (resulting in Facebook's default shadow head image where your picture should be), mouse over your profile picture, click **Edit Profile Picture**, and then select **Remove**. ■

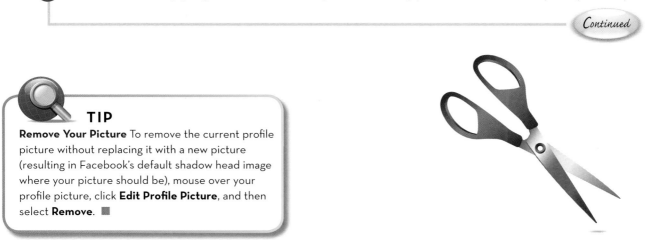

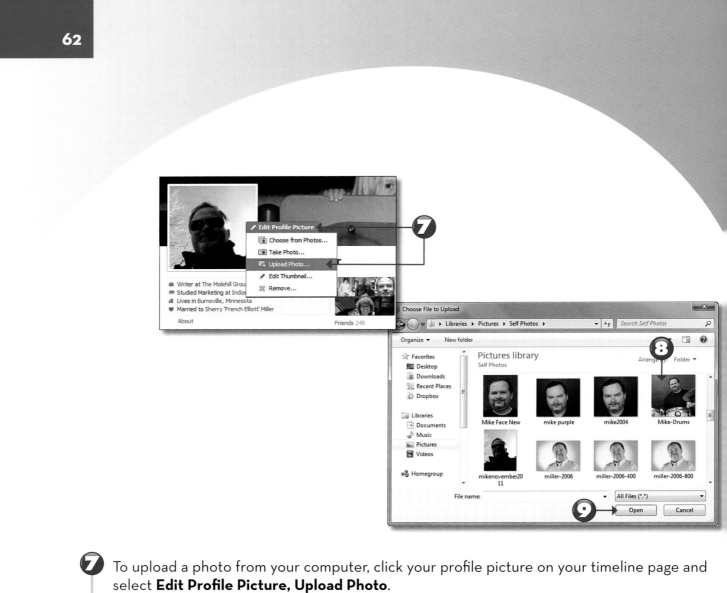

**7** To upload a photo from your computer, click your profile picture on your timeline page and select **Edit Profile Picture, Upload Photo**.

**8** When the Choose File to Upload or Open dialog box appears, navigate to and select the photo you want.

**9** Click the **Open** button. The selected photo is now used as your profile photo.

*Continued*

**TIP**

**Setting Any Photo for Your Profile** You can set any photo you've uploaded to Facebook as your profile picture. Navigate to and display the photo within your photo albums and then click the **Options** button and select **Make Profile Picture**. ■

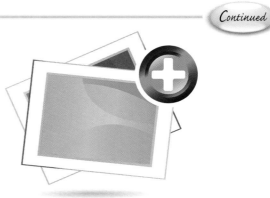

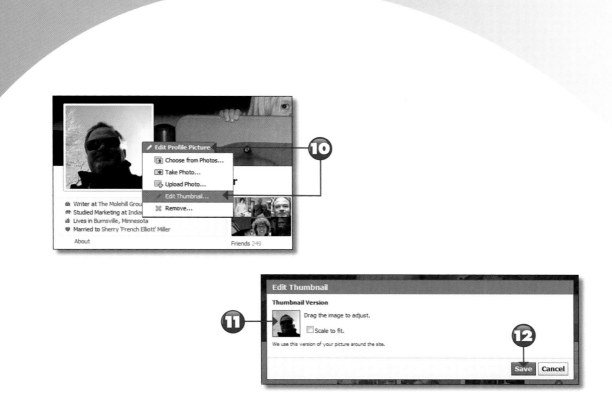

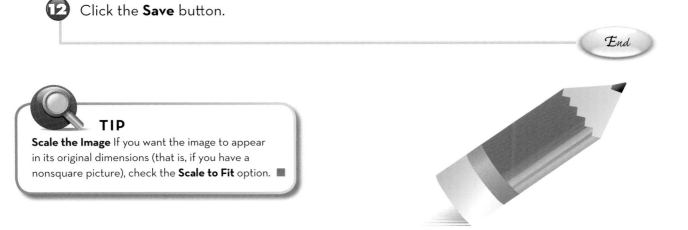

**10** To edit the thumbnail version of the picture used as your profile picture, click your profile photo on your timeline page and select **Edit Profile Picture, Edit Thumbnail**.

**11** When the Edit Thumbnail dialog box appears, drag the image until it looks like you want it to.

**12** Click the **Save** button.

End

**TIP**

**Scale the Image** If you want the image to appear in its original dimensions (that is, if you have a nonsquare picture), check the **Scale to Fit** option. ■

# ADDING A COVER IMAGE

By default, your profile picture appears against a blue tinted background on your timeline page. You can, however, select a background image (called a *cover*) to appear on the top of the page.

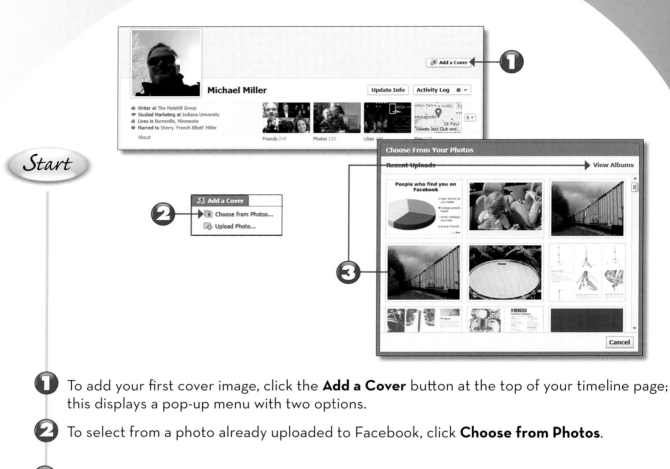

1. To add your first cover image, click the **Add a Cover** button at the top of your timeline page; this displays a pop-up menu with two options.

2. To select from a photo already uploaded to Facebook, click **Choose from Photos**.

3. When the Choose from Your Photos dialog box appears, click one of the photos or click **View Albums** to select a photo from one of your photo albums.

*Continued*

 **TIP**

**Change Your Cover** To change an existing cover image, mouse over the image and click the **Change Cover** button. ■

 **TIP**

**Appropriate Images** When choosing a cover image, make sure you choose an image that's wider than it is tall and one that looks good in this landscape orientation. If you want to specifically size the image, Facebook's cover is 851 pixels wide by 315 pixels tall. If you upload a smaller image, Facebook will stretch it to fill the space. (Your image must be at least 399 pixels wide to work.) ■

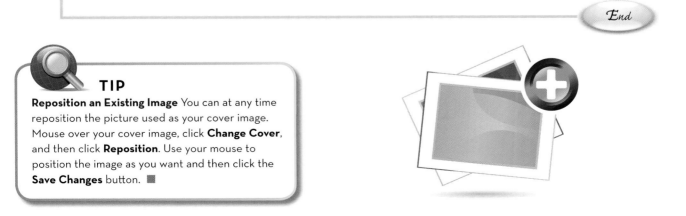

**4** To select a photo stored on your computer, click the **Add a Cover** button and then click the **Upload a Photo** option.

**5** When the Choose File to Upload or Open dialog box appears, navigate to and select the picture you want to use and then click the **Open** button.

**6** You're now prompted to drag to reposition the cover image. Use your mouse to position the image appropriately.

**7** Click the **Save Changes** button when done.

*End*

**TIP**

**Reposition an Existing Image** You can at any time reposition the picture used as your cover image. Mouse over your cover image, click **Change Cover**, and then click **Reposition**. Use your mouse to position the image as you want and then click the **Save Changes** button. ∎

# PERSONALIZING TOP-OF-PAGE ELEMENTS

Just beneath your cover image, Facebook displays several graphical elements, for Photos, Friends, and such. You can change the order of these elements and even display additional elements if you like.

① Click the **down arrow** at the far right of the row of elements. This opens each item for editing.

② To move an element to a new position, mouse over the item, click the **pencil** icon, and then select the element you want to swap position with.

③ To remove an element from your timeline page, mouse over the item, click the **pencil** icon, and then click **Remove from Favorites.**

Continued

## NOTE

**Elements, Apps, and Tabs** In the old pre-timeline days, these top-of-page elements were displayed on individual tabs on the profile page. With the advent of the timeline, Facebook consolidated each tab into its own graphical element, which it calls *apps*. (Not to be confused with the discrete apps and games discussed in Chapter 11, "Working with Facebook Pages, Apps, and Games.") ■

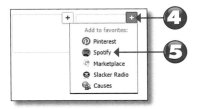

**4** To add a new element to the row, click the **+** button on an empty box beneath the existing elements to display a list of choices.

**5** Click the new element you want to add.

*End*

**CAUTION**

**Unremovable and Immovable** You cannot move or remove the default Friends and Photos elements. ■

# HIDING AND DELETING STATUS UPDATES

The main section of your timeline displays all the status updates you've made on Facebook. That doesn't mean you need to display every single status update, however; if there's an embarrassing update out there, you can choose to hide it. You can also delete the worst of these updates.

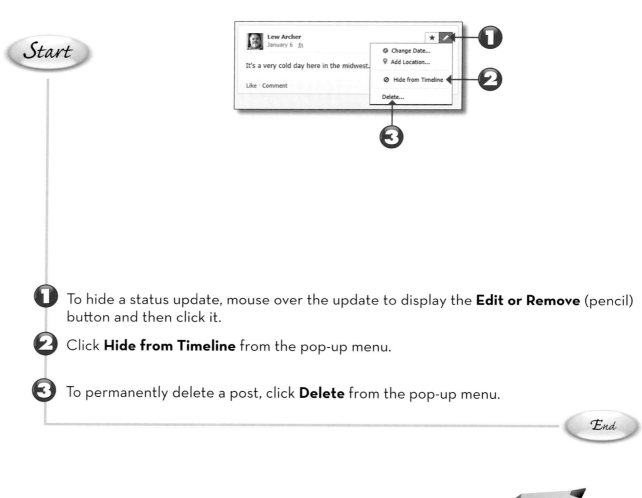

**Start**

① To hide a status update, mouse over the update to display the **Edit or Remove** (pencil) button and then click it.

② Click **Hide from Timeline** from the pop-up menu.

③ To permanently delete a post, click **Delete** from the pop-up menu.

**End**

**CAUTION**

**Can't Delete 'em All** Not all status updates can be deleted. If the **Delete** option doesn't appear, opt to hide the update instead. ■

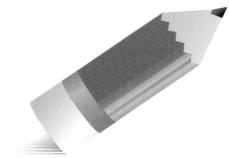

# HIGHLIGHTING YOUR FAVORITE STATUS UPDATES

By default, each status updates are displayed in one of the two columns on your timeline page. You can highlight your favorite or most important updates, however, which displays them across the full two-column width of the page.

Start

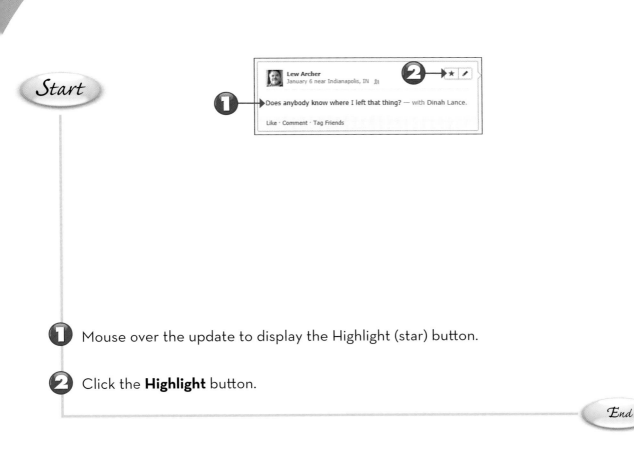

① Mouse over the update to display the Highlight (star) button.

② Click the **Highlight** button.

End

**TIP**

**Unfeaturing an Update** To "unfeature" a post and return it to single-column display, just click the **Highlight** button again. ■

# VIEWING AND EDITING YOUR ACTIVITY LOG

Your timeline page presents all your Facebook activity in a nice, visually attractive fashion. However, if you want a more straightforward view of what you've done online, you can display and edit Facebook's Activity Log, which lists every little thing you've done on the Facebook site, from status updates to links to comments to you name it.

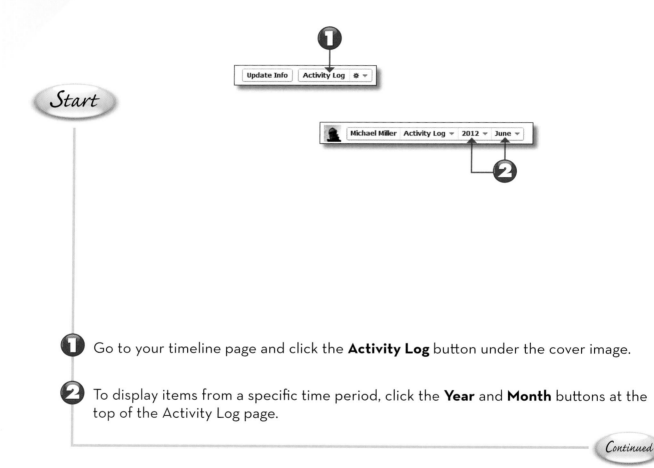

*Start*

1. Go to your timeline page and click the **Activity Log** button under the cover image.

2. To display items from a specific time period, click the **Year** and **Month** buttons at the top of the Activity Log page.

*Continued*

**TIP**

**Clean Up Your Timeline** Many users find the Activity Log a more efficient way to clean up entries on your timeline. It's easier to see what's posted (and available to post) from the more condensed Activity Log listing. ■

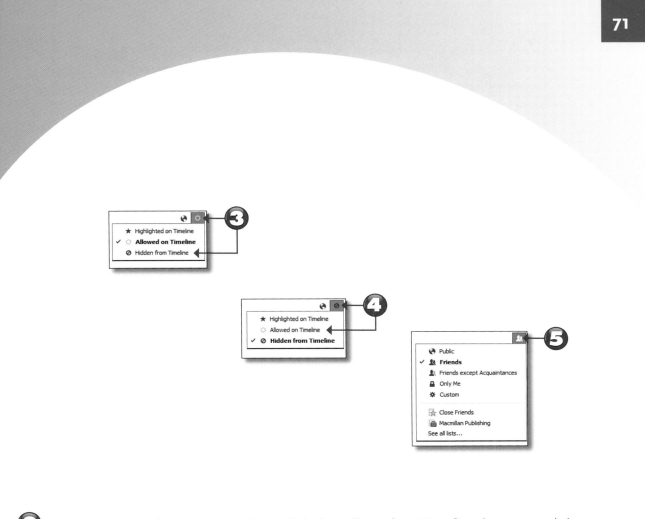

**3** To hide an item from your timeline, click the **Allowed on Timeline** button, and then click **Hidden from Timeline**.

**4** To redisplay a hidden item on your timeline, click the **Hidden from Timeline** button, and then click **Allowed on Timeline**.

**5** To change who can view an item, click the **Privacy** button and select from **Public**, **Friends**, **Friends Except Acquaintances**, **Only Me**, or **Custom**.

End

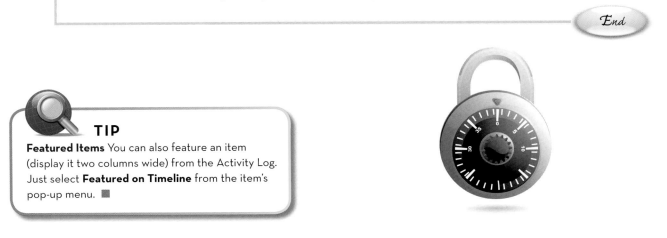

### TIP

**Featured Items** You can also feature an item (display it two columns wide) from the Activity Log. Just select **Featured on Timeline** from the item's pop-up menu. ■

# ADDING LIFE EVENTS TO YOUR TIMELINE

Facebook's intention with the timeline is to tell the "story of your life" on a single page. But Facebook can only display those events it knows about, from what you've entered into your personal profile. You can, however, supplement this information by adding other milestones, what Facebook calls *life events*, to your timeline.

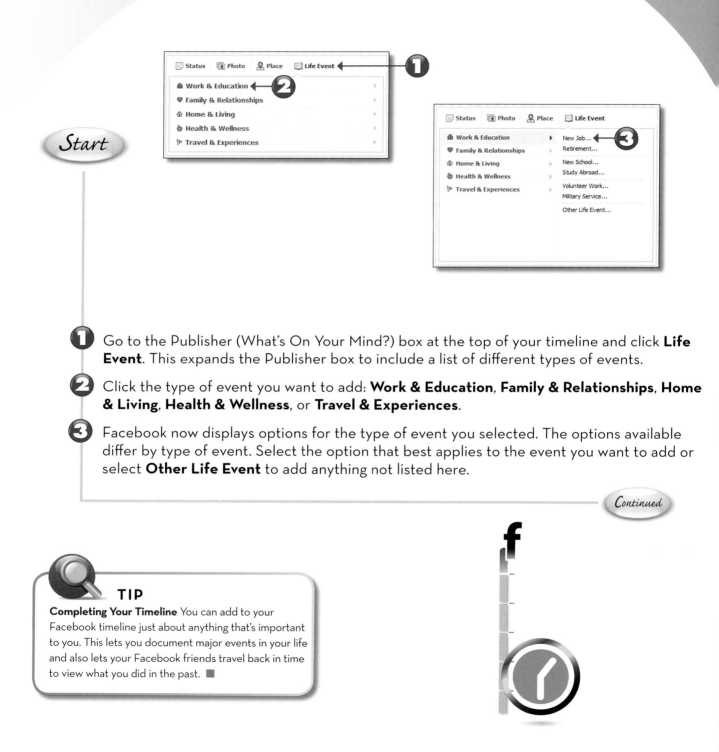

Go to the Publisher (What's On Your Mind?) box at the top of your timeline and click **Life Event**. This expands the Publisher box to include a list of different types of events.

Click the type of event you want to add: **Work & Education**, **Family & Relationships**, **Home & Living**, **Health & Wellness**, or **Travel & Experiences**.

Facebook now displays options for the type of event you selected. The options available differ by type of event. Select the option that best applies to the event you want to add or select **Other Life Event** to add anything not listed here.

Continued

**TIP**

**Completing Your Timeline** You can add to your Facebook timeline just about anything that's important to you. This lets you document major events in your life and also lets your Facebook friends travel back in time to view what you did in the past. ■

**Started a Job**
2012

**4**

| | |
|---|---|
| Employer | |
| Position | Optional |
| Location | ⊙ Optional |
| | ☑ I currently work here |
| When | 2012 ▾ + Add month to present. |
| Story | Optional |

Choose from Photos... ◄—— **5**

Upload Photo... ◄

**6**

To edit who can see your work history, go to your About view. [Save] [Cancel]

**4** You now see a panel specific to the type of event you selected. For example, if you opted to enter a new job, you see the Started a Job panel, with fields for Employer, Position, Location, When, and so forth. Enter the appropriate information for this event.

**5** In many instances, there is the opportunity to add photos related to the event. Click **Upload Photo** to choose pictures stored on your computer or **Choose from Photos** to select pictures previously uploaded to a Facebook photo album.

**6** Click the **Save** button when done. The event is now posted to your timeline.

*End*

### TIP

**Adding Events Directly** Alternatively, you can add new life events directly to your timeline. Just scroll to a specific location on the timeline and hover your cursor over that point in the middle line; your cursor will turn into a plus (+) sign. Click the center line and, when the pop-up appears, click **Life Event**. Continue from this point by selecting the type of event and so forth, as just described. ■

### CAUTION

**Use Discretion** You should use discretion when adding milestones to your timeline; be aware of what you do or don't want others to know about your life. For example, do you really want current or future employers knowing when you smoked your first joint, or your spouse knowing about each and every intimate relationship you had prior to getting married? Use your own best judgment, but err on the side of being discrete. ■

# UPDATING YOUR PROFILE INFORMATION

Facebook also lets you edit or add to the personal information in your Facebook profile. You can also select who can view what information in your profile.

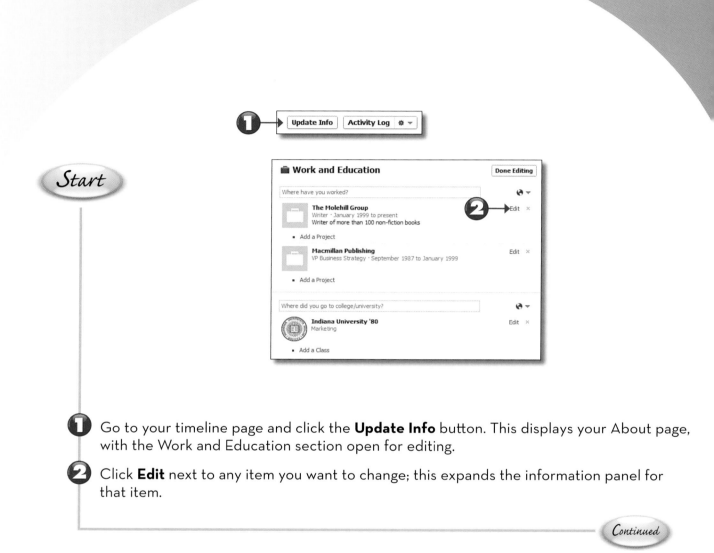

Start

① Go to your timeline page and click the **Update Info** button. This displays your About page, with the Work and Education section open for editing.

② Click **Edit** next to any item you want to change; this expands the information panel for that item.

Continued

### TIP

**It's All Optional** All the personal information that Facebook requests is optional. Know, however, that the more Facebook knows about you, the better it can suggest appropriate activities and match you with potential friends. ■

**3** Edit the information as necessary.

**4** Click **Save Changes** to save your edits for this item.

Continued

**TIP**

**Finding Friends** To increase the number of potential friends that Facebook suggests for you, make sure you add every school you attended and every employer you worked for to your profile information. ■

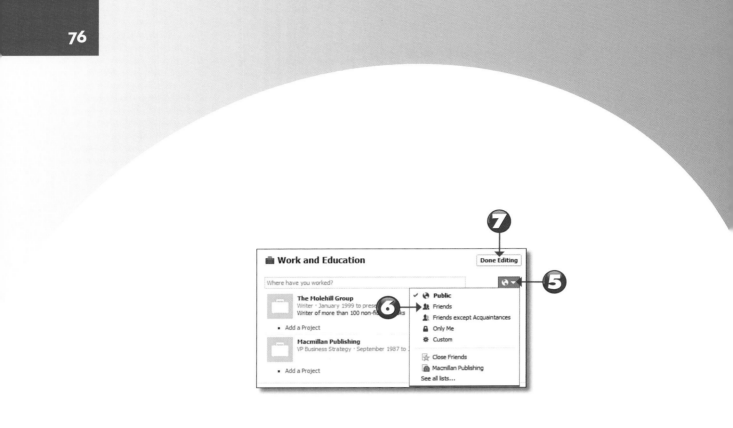

5. To determine who can see a given piece of information, click the **Privacy** button next to that item.

6. Select who can view this information: **Public**, **Friends**, **Friends Except Acquaintances**, **Only Me**, or **Custom**.

7. Click **Done Editing** to close editing on this section.

Continued

**CAUTION**

**Who Knows What?** Not everyone viewing your profile needs to see all your information. For example, you might want everyone to view your birthdate, but not necessarily the year of your birth. You may want only your friends to view your marital status or want to share your personal contact information with no one. You can fine-tune your profile as granularly as you like, in this fashion. ■

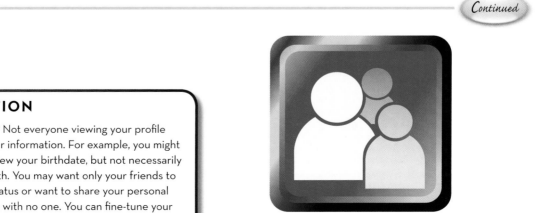

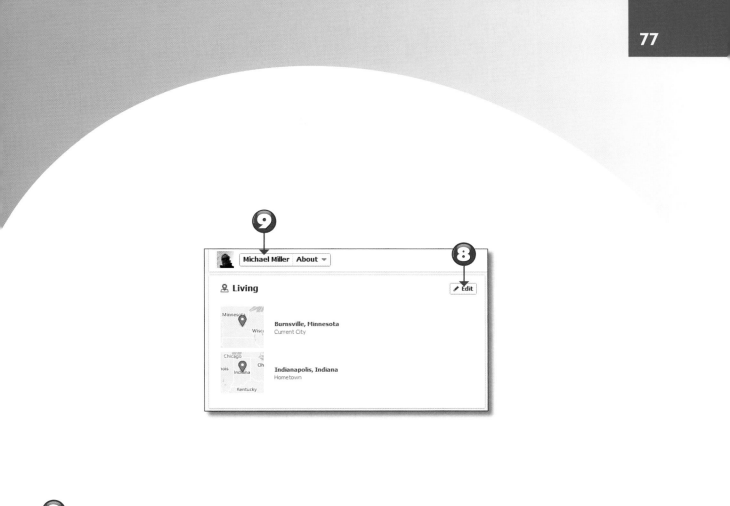

**8** To edit another section of your profile, click the **Edit** button for that section.

**9** To return to your timeline page, click your name at the top of this page.

*End*

**NOTE**

**Timeline Controversy** If you're new to Facebook, all you know is the timeline. But the timeline is a relatively new addition; before this, everyone had a somewhat simple profile page. Some Facebook users did not react well to the imposition of the timeline and how easy it makes it to find individual status updates. These users continue to voice their protests today. ∎

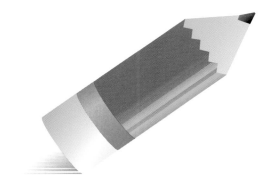

## Chapter 7

# ORGANIZING YOUR FRIENDS INTO LISTS

After you've been on Facebook for any length of time, you'll find that you've added quite a few people to your friends list. Between old friends from your youth, current friends and co-workers, and assorted family members, you might end up with anywhere from a few dozen to a few hundred Facebook friends.

The problem with having so many friends on Facebook, however, is managing them; that's a lot of people to track in your news feed. The solution is to organize your friends into custom lists within your main list. It's a great way to send posts, photos, chats, and other files to selected friends only, instead of your entire friends list—and to simplify your news feed, by viewing only posts from specific lists of friends.

For example, you might want to create a list that contains only family members. Or you could create a list of people you currently work with. You can also create a list for people on your son's basketball team or in your daughter's gymnastics class. You can create a list for your book club, church group, or community group. You can even create lists for collaborative projects, such as for a class or business project.

# VIEWING FRIENDS LISTS

Click to view list
news feed

Click to create
new list

List suggestions

Click to remove
list

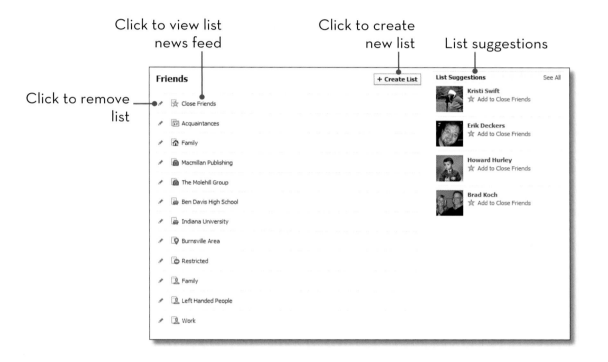

# VIEWING YOUR FRIENDS LISTS AND POSTS

One of the benefits of friends lists is making it easy to read only those updates from list members. All your friends lists are displayed in the Friends section of the left sidebar on the Facebook home page.

**Start**

**1** Go to the Friends section of the left sidebar and click a list to view the news feed for that list.

**2** Comment on a post as you would normally.

**3** Mouse over the Friends section header and click **More** to view all your friends lists.

*Continued*

### TIP
**More** If you don't see the Friends section in the left sidebar, click **More** to display this and additional sections. ■

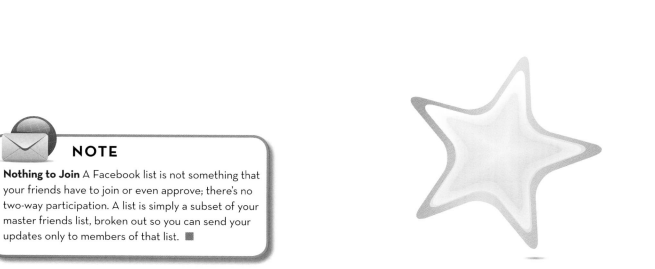

**4** Click a list to view the news feed for that list.

End

**NOTE**

**Nothing to Join** A Facebook list is not something that your friends have to join or even approve; there's no two-way participation. A list is simply a subset of your master friends list, broken out so you can send your updates only to members of that list. ■

# CREATING A NEW FRIENDS LIST

To get the most out of Facebook's friends lists, you'll want to create your own custom lists. You can create as many tightly focused lists as you like.

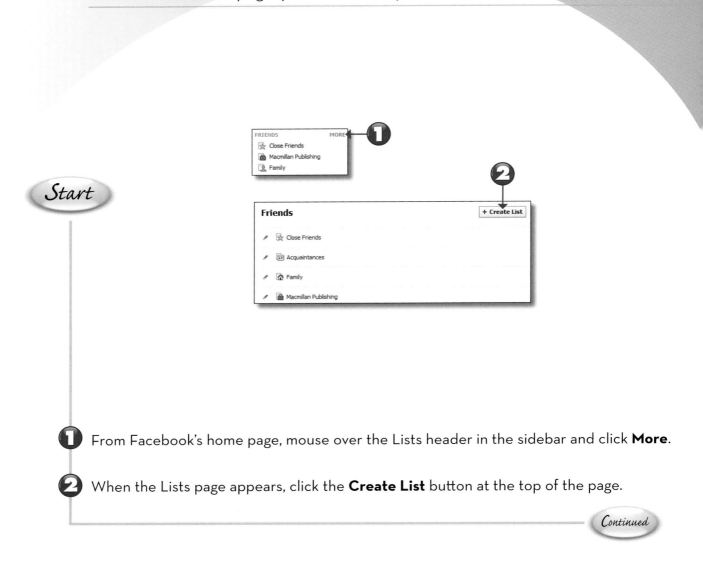

**Start**

**1** From Facebook's home page, mouse over the Lists header in the sidebar and click **More**.

**2** When the Lists page appears, click the **Create List** button at the top of the page.

*Continued*

---

**TIP**

**Smart Lists** To help you get started with friends lists, Facebook creates a handful of automatic lists for you, which it calls *smart lists*. The three default smart lists are Close Friends, Acquaintances, and Family. In addition, Facebook may create smart lists based on your work, school, and local affiliations. For example, if you work at Fidelity Insurance, you might see a Fidelity Insurance list, prepopulated with other co-workers. ■

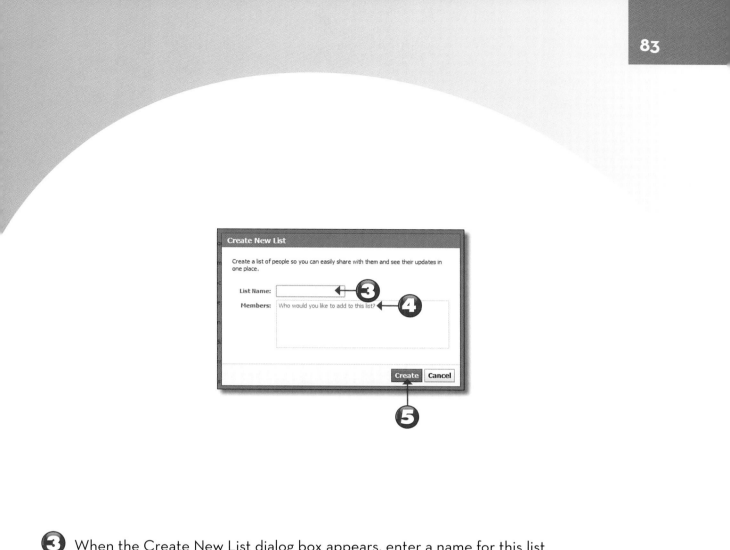

**3** When the Create New List dialog box appears, enter a name for this list.

**4** If you want to add members to this list now, type their names into the Members box.

**5** Click the **Create** button

End

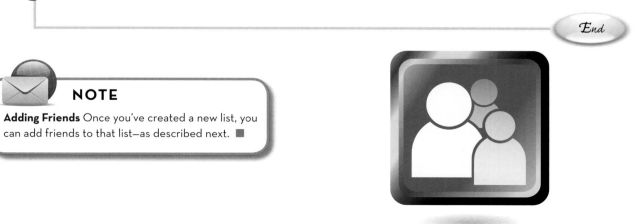

**NOTE**

**Adding Friends** Once you've created a new list, you can add friends to that list—as described next. ■

# ADDING FRIENDS TO A LIST

There are two ways to add friends to a list: from the friend's timeline page or from your own list page. We'll examine how to add friends from your list page.

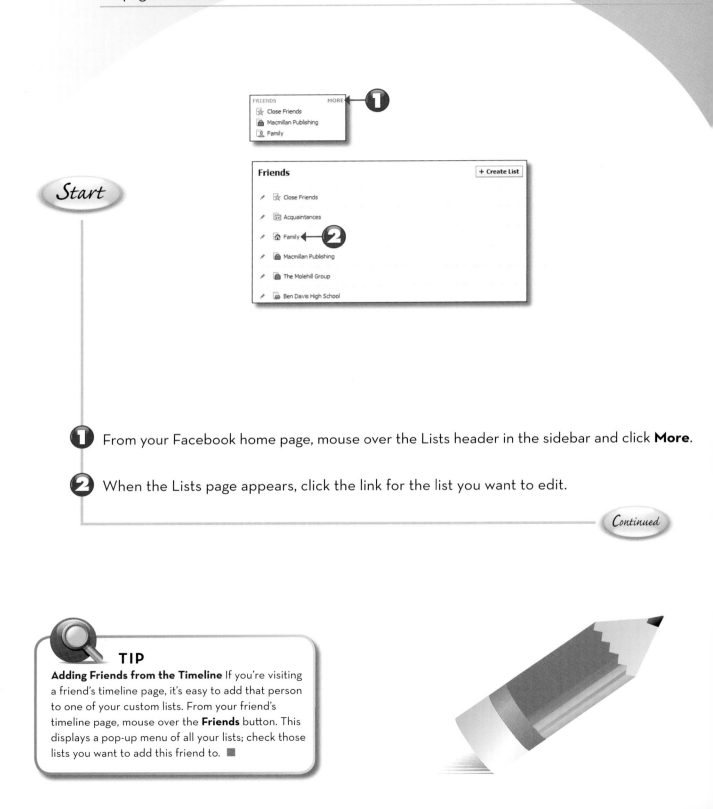

**Start**

**1** From your Facebook home page, mouse over the Lists header in the sidebar and click **More**.

**2** When the Lists page appears, click the link for the list you want to edit.

Continued

---

## TIP

**Adding Friends from the Timeline** If you're visiting a friend's timeline page, it's easy to add that person to one of your custom lists. From your friend's timeline page, mouse over the **Friends** button. This displays a pop-up menu of all your lists; check those lists you want to add this friend to. ■

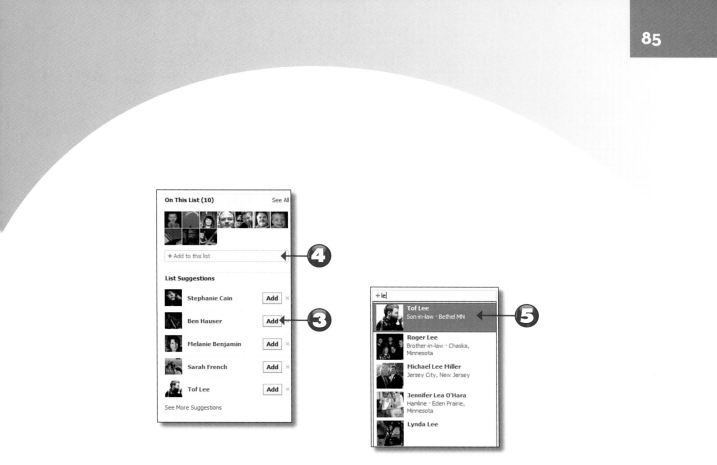

**3** When the list page appears, you see a list of suggested friends in the right column. To add one of these people to the list, click the **Add** button next to his or her name.

**4** To add other friends to this list, enter their names into the Add to This List box.

**5** Matching friends will appear in a drop-down list; click a friend to add him or her to your list.

*End*

 **CAUTION**

**Too Many Close Friends** Be careful about putting too many people into Facebook's default Close Friends list. By default, Facebook notifies you every time someone on this list posts a new status update; too many "close friends" and you could get inundated with updates and notifications. ■

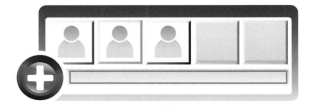

# REMOVING A FRIEND FROM A LIST

What do you do if you accidentally place someone in the wrong list—or later decide you don't want to include an individual in that list? It's easy to remove any given person from a Facebook list.

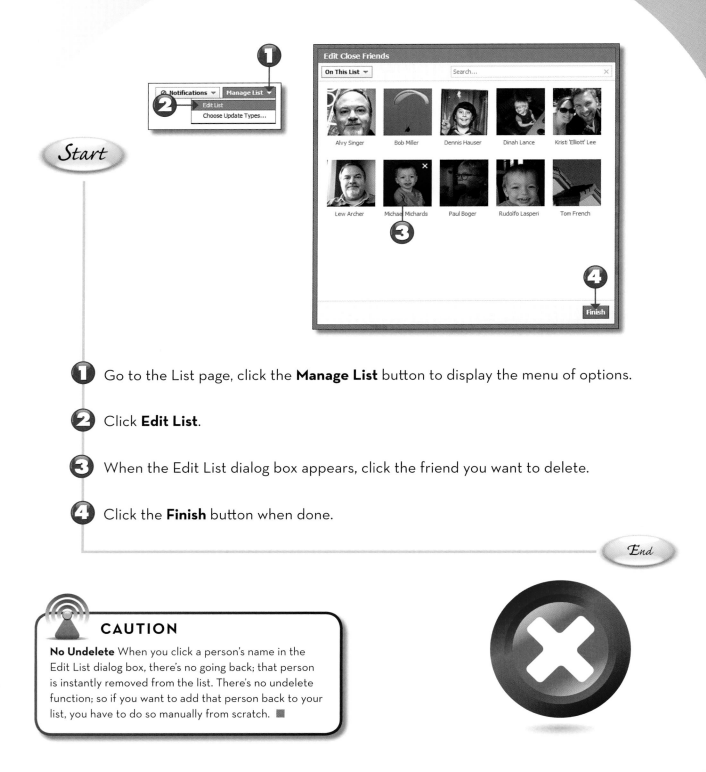

Start

**1** Go to the List page, click the **Manage List** button to display the menu of options.

**2** Click **Edit List**.

**3** When the Edit List dialog box appears, click the friend you want to delete.

**4** Click the **Finish** button when done.

End

## CAUTION

**No Undelete** When you click a person's name in the Edit List dialog box, there's no going back; that person is instantly removed from the list. There's no undelete function; so if you want to add that person back to your list, you have to do so manually from scratch. ■

# POSTING TO A LIST

When you're creating a new status update, you can opt to post only to members of a given list. It's easy to do.

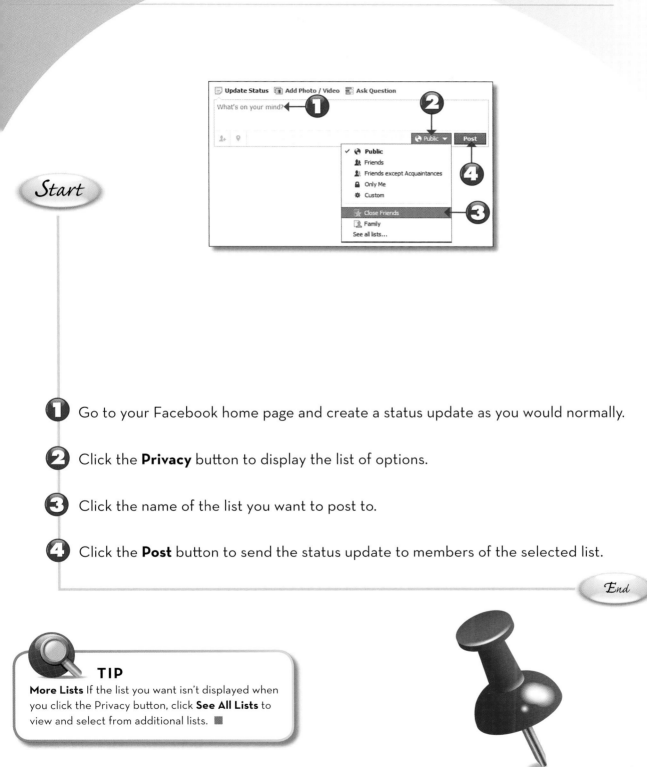

**Start**

**1** Go to your Facebook home page and create a status update as you would normally.

**2** Click the **Privacy** button to display the list of options.

**3** Click the name of the list you want to post to.

**4** Click the **Post** button to send the status update to members of the selected list.

**End**

**TIP**

**More Lists** If the list you want isn't displayed when you click the Privacy button, click **See All Lists** to view and select from additional lists. ■

## Chapter 8

# SHARING PICTURES

Sharing pictures is a great way to catch up your friends and family on what you've been up to. In the old days, you had to make photo prints and mail them out to everyone, or invite everybody over for an old-fashioned slide show. Today, however, you can share your photos online—via Facebook.

Facebook is the largest photo-sharing site on the Internet. It's easy to upload photos to a Facebook photo album and then share them with all your Facebook friends. It's equally easy to view your friends' photos on Facebook and download and print those you'd like to keep.

You can post just about any kind of photo to your Facebook account. As long as your photo is in one of the popular file types (JPG, PNG, GIF, TIFF, or BMP), is no larger than 15MB in size, doesn't contain any adult or offensive content, and you own it (that is, you haven't copied the photo from another person's website), you should be good to go.

# VIEWING A PHOTO

When photo was posted

Person who posted photo

Close photo lightbox

Description

People tagged in this photo

View previous photo

View next photo

Tag people in this photo

Like this photo

Download photo or view fullscreen

Share photo on your timeline

Comment on photo

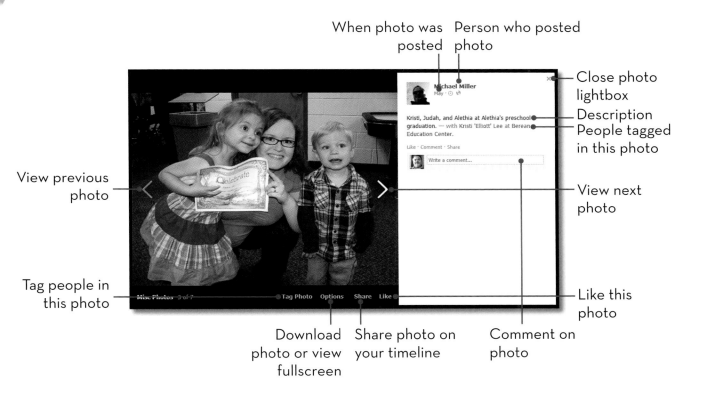

## VIEWING A FRIEND'S PHOTOS

Facebook makes it easy to view photos that your friends post on their accounts. You can navigate through a friend's photo albums to find and view the photos you like.

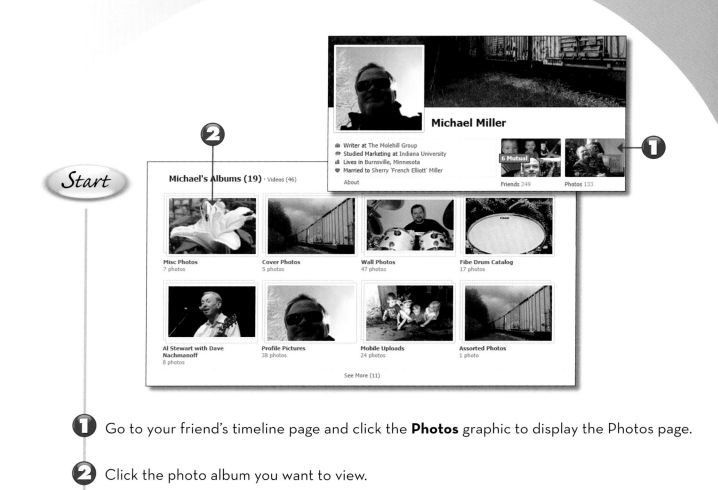

*Start*

**1** Go to your friend's timeline page and click the **Photos** graphic to display the Photos page.

**2** Click the photo album you want to view.

*Continued*

**TIP**

**See More** The top of the Photos page displays your friend's most recent albums. Click **See More** to view all albums your friend has created. ■

**NOTE**

**Photos of Your Friend** The bottom of the Photos page displays photos and videos in which your friend has been tagged—either in her own photo albums or in photos uploaded by other users. ■

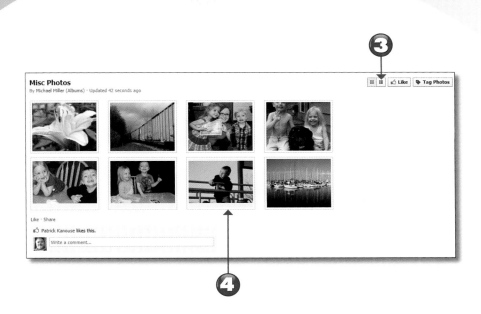

**3** By default, pictures in an album are displayed in Album View. To switch to what Facebook calls Comment View, click the **Comment View** button at the top right of the album.

**4** Click the thumbnail of the picture you want to view.

Continued

**NOTE**

**Comment View** In Comment View, you can read a photo's description and comment on and like a photo directly from the album page. ■

**TIP**

**Commenting on an Album** Facebook lets you comment on individual photos or on complete albums. To comment on an album, display the album page and then enter your comments into the Write a Comment box at the bottom of the page. ■

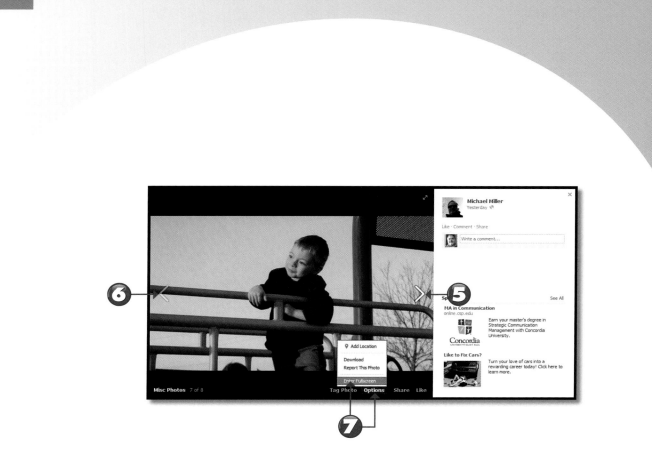

**5** Facebook now displays the selected picture in a *lightbox* superimposed on top of the previous page. To go to the next picture in the album, mouse over the current picture to display the navigational arrows and then click the **right arrow**.

**6** To go to the previous picture, mouse over the current picture to display the navigational arrows and then click the **left arrow**.

**7** To view the photo fullscreen, mouse over the picture to display the bottom menus and click **Options**, **Enter Fullscreen**.

*Continued*

**NOTE**

**Photo Description** Your friend's description of the photo is displayed to the right of the photo lightbox viewer. If no description appears, your friend didn't enter one. ■

**CAUTION**

**Fullscreen Mode** The fullscreen option is not available with all web browsers. At the time of this writing, only Chrome and Firefox browsers has the fullscreen option; Internet Explorer does not. ■

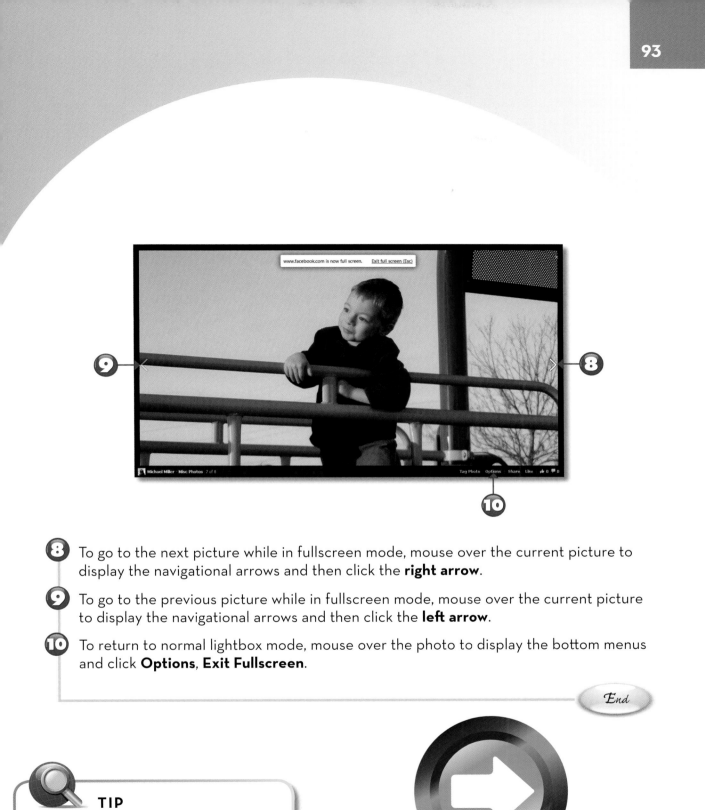

**8** To go to the next picture while in fullscreen mode, mouse over the current picture to display the navigational arrows and then click the **right arrow**.

**9** To go to the previous picture while in fullscreen mode, mouse over the current picture to display the navigational arrows and then click the **left arrow**.

**10** To return to normal lightbox mode, mouse over the photo to display the bottom menus and click **Options**, **Exit Fullscreen**.

*End*

**TIP**

**Escape Fullscreen Mode** You can also exit fullscreen mode by pressing the **Esc** button on your computer keyboard. ■

# ADDING YOUR COMMENTS TO A FRIEND'S PHOTO

If you'd like to say something about a given photo, enter your comments on the photo page. Your comments will now appear when others view this photo.

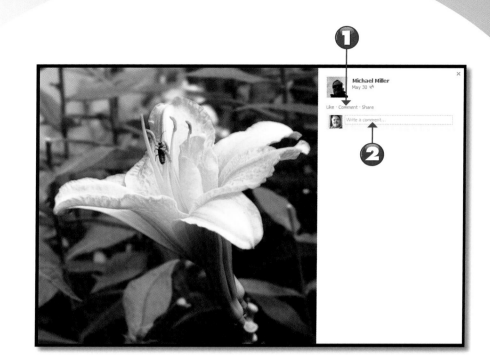

1 Go to the photo page and click the **Comment** link to the right of the photo viewer.

2 Enter your comments into the Write a Comment box and then press **Enter** when done.

**TIP**

**Liking a Photo** You can also "like" a photo without entering full comments about it. When you're viewing a photo, click the **Like** link to the right of the photo viewer. ■

# SHARING A FRIEND'S PHOTO

If you really like a given photo, you can share that photo on your own timeline—with your own description.

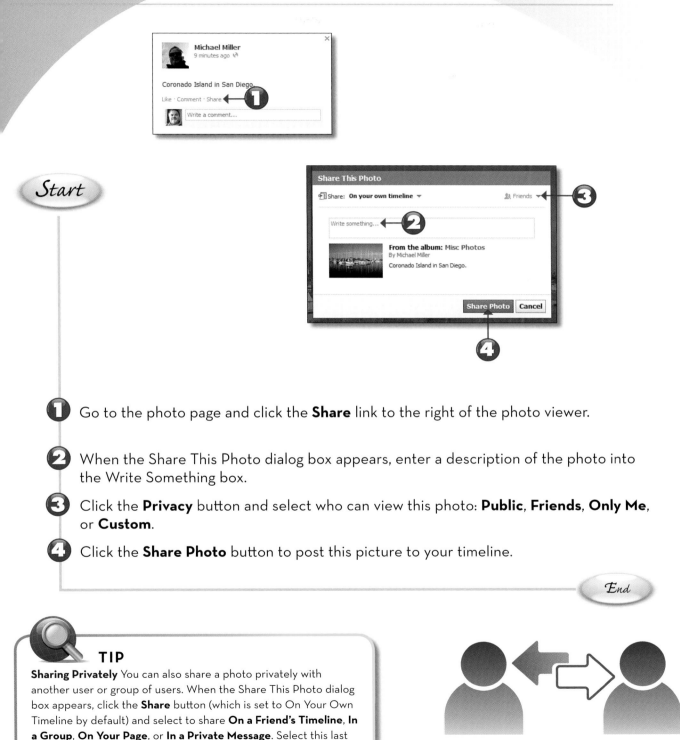

**Start**

**End**

1.  Go to the photo page and click the **Share** link to the right of the photo viewer.

2.  When the Share This Photo dialog box appears, enter a description of the photo into the Write Something box.

3.  Click the **Privacy** button and select who can view this photo: **Public**, **Friends**, **Only Me**, or **Custom**.

4.  Click the **Share Photo** button to post this picture to your timeline.

## TIP

**Sharing Privately** You can also share a photo privately with another user or group of users. When the Share This Photo dialog box appears, click the **Share** button (which is set to On Your Own Timeline by default) and select to share **On a Friend's Timeline**, **In a Group**, **On Your Page**, or **In a Private Message**. Select this last option to share the photo with a specific individual. ■

# TAGGING YOURSELF IN A FRIEND'S PHOTO

If you find yourself in a photo that a friend has taken and uploaded to Facebook, you can "tag" yourself in that photo. This identifies you in that photo.

**Start**

**1** Go to the photo page and mouse over the photo to display the menu at the bottom of the photo.

**2** Click **Tag Photo**.

Continued

## NOTE

**Tags** When you're tagged in a photo, that photo appears in your Facebook timeline and on your Facebook photo albums page in the Photos and Videos of You section. ■

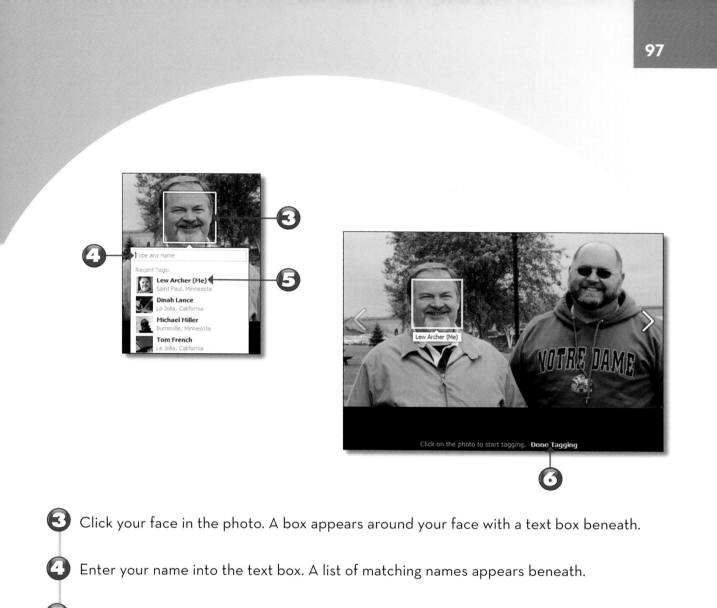

**3** Click your face in the photo. A box appears around your face with a text box beneath.

**4** Enter your name into the text box. A list of matching names appears beneath.

**5** Click your name in the list.

**6** Your name is now tagged to your face in this photo. Click **Done Tagging** to finish.

End

### TIP

**Remove a Tag** You may not want to be tagged in a given picture. To remove a tag, open the page for that photo, mouse over the photo to display the bottom menu, and then select **Options**, **Report/Remove Tag**. When the next dialog box appears, check **I Want to Remove Tag** and then click the **Continue** button. ■

# DOWNLOADING A FRIEND'S PHOTO

If you find a friend's photo that you really like, you can download it to your own computer, for your own use.

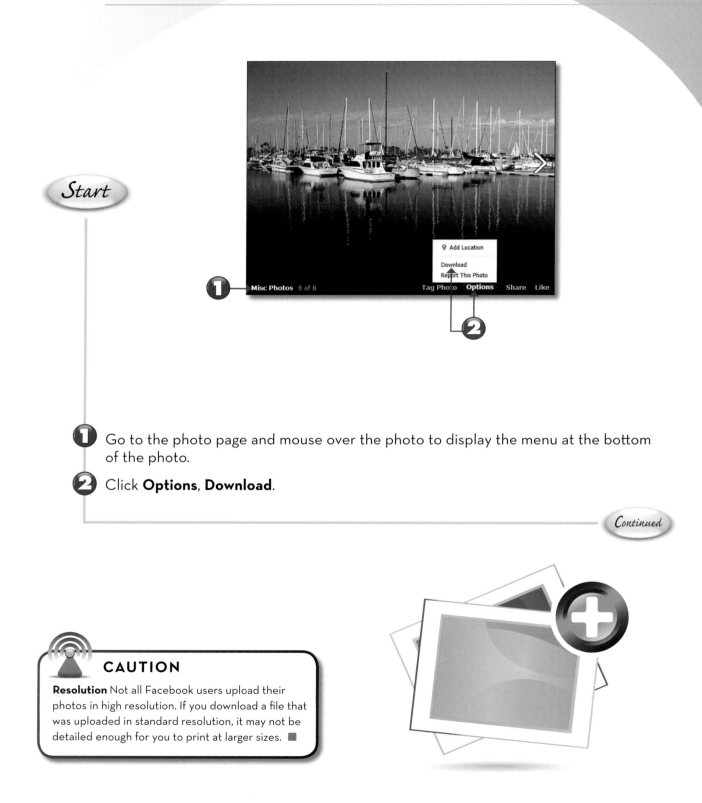

*Start*

**1** Go to the photo page and mouse over the photo to display the menu at the bottom of the photo.

**2** Click **Options**, **Download**.

*Continued*

## CAUTION

**Resolution** Not all Facebook users upload their photos in high resolution. If you download a file that was uploaded in standard resolution, it may not be detailed enough for you to print at larger sizes. ■

③ If you're prompted to open or save the file, click **Save**.

④ If you see the Save As dialog box, select where you want to save the file and then click the **Save** button.

*End*

### CAUTION

**Copyright** When you download a photo from Facebook, you do not own that photo. The copyright on that photo is owned by the person who originally took or uploaded the photo, which means you cannot use that photo for anything other than your own personal purposes. ■

# PRINTING A FRIEND'S PHOTO

Facebook does not have a "print" button for the photos on its site. You can, however, print a photo directly from its Facebook page using the print feature in your web browser.

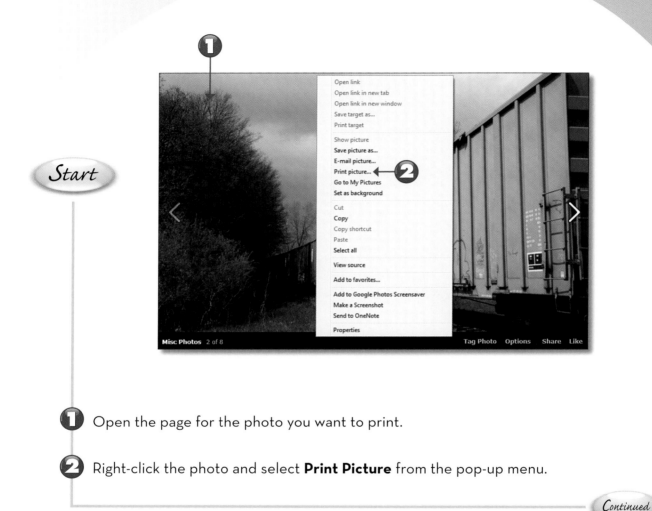

1. Open the page for the photo you want to print.

2. Right-click the photo and select **Print Picture** from the pop-up menu.

Continued

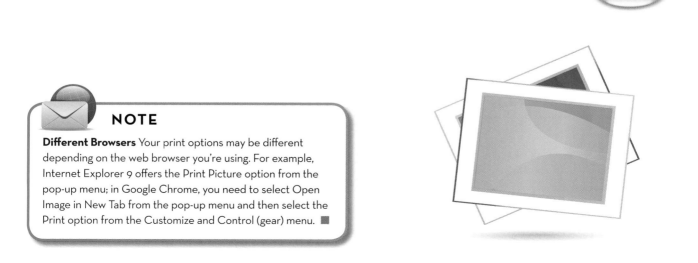

## NOTE

**Different Browsers** Your print options may be different depending on the web browser you're using. For example, Internet Explorer 9 offers the Print Picture option from the pop-up menu; in Google Chrome, you need to select Open Image in New Tab from the pop-up menu and then select the Print option from the Customize and Control (gear) menu. ■

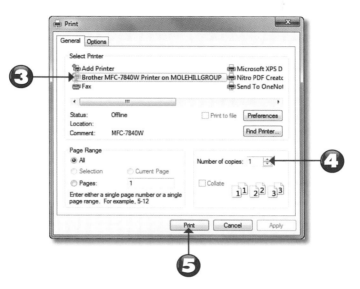

**3** When the Print dialog box appears, select the printer you want to use.

**4** Select how many copies you want to print.

**5** Click the **Print** button.

End

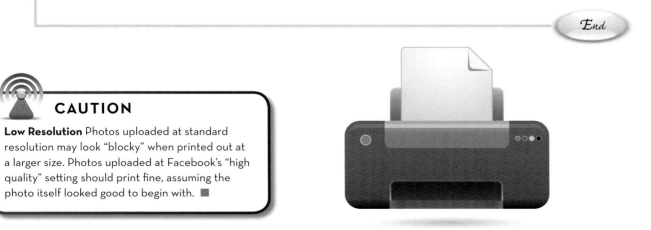

### CAUTION

**Low Resolution** Photos uploaded at standard resolution may look "blocky" when printed out at a larger size. Photos uploaded at Facebook's "high quality" setting should print fine, assuming the photo itself looked good to begin with. ■

# UPLOADING YOUR PICTURES TO A NEW PHOTO ALBUM

It's relatively easy to upload and share your own pictures on the Facebook site. You can upload new photos to an existing photo album or create a new album for newly uploaded photos.

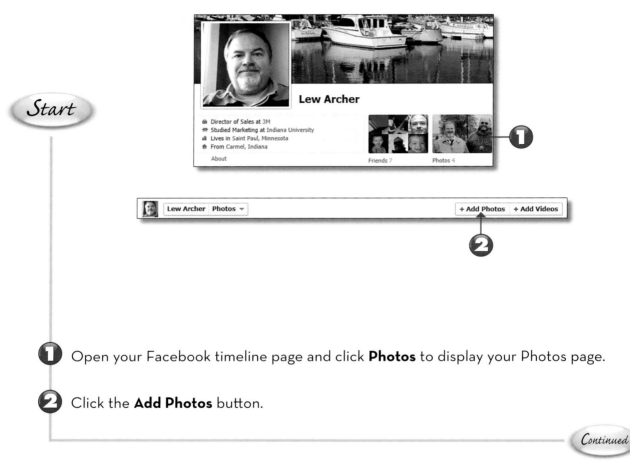

*Start*

**1** Open your Facebook timeline page and click **Photos** to display your Photos page.

**2** Click the **Add Photos** button.

*Continued*

### TIP

**Photo Albums** Take advantage of Facebook's photo albums feature and create multiple topic-specific photo albums for the photos you upload. For example, you might create an album for Summer Vacation 2012, Christmas 2013, or Ben's Senior Hockey Team. This makes it easier for your friends to find specific photos. ■

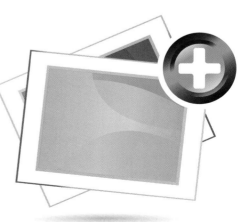

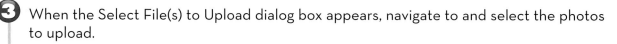

**3** When the Select File(s) to Upload dialog box appears, navigate to and select the photos to upload.

**4** Click the **Open** button.

Continued

**TIP**

**Multiple Photos** You can upload more than one photo at a time. Hold down the **Ctrl** key while clicking files to select multiple files. ■

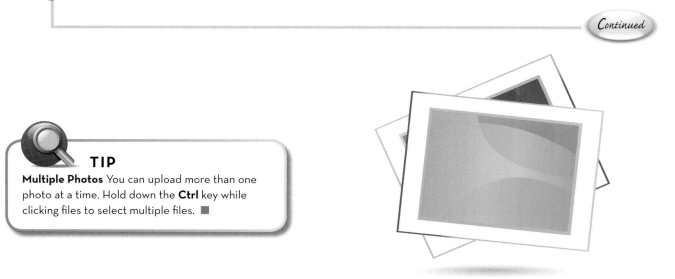

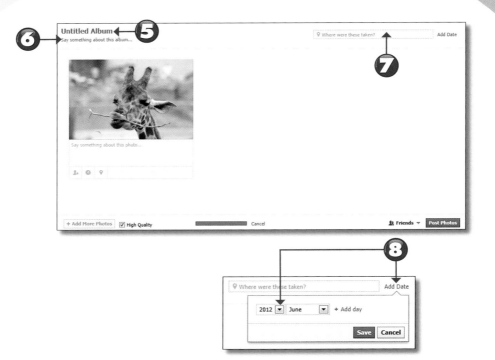

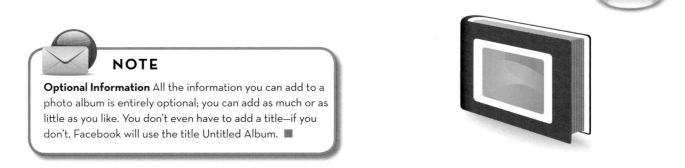

**5** You now see the Untitled Album page. Click **Untitled Album** and enter the desired album title.

**6** Click **Say Something About This Album** and enter an album description.

**7** To enter a geographic location for all the photos in this album, go to the Where Were These Taken? box and enter a location.

**8** To add a date to all the photos in this album, click **Add Date** and select a date from the pop-up box.

*Continued*

**NOTE**

**Optional Information** All the information you can add to a photo album is entirely optional; you can add as much or as little as you like. You don't even have to add a title—if you don't, Facebook will use the title Untitled Album.

105

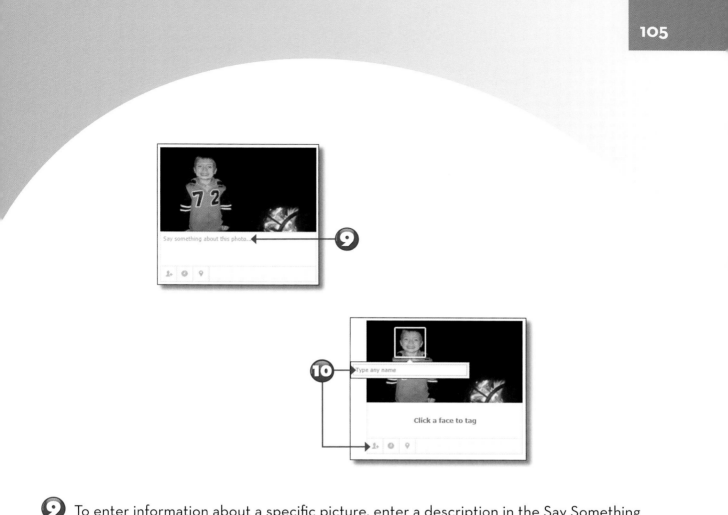

**9** To enter information about a specific picture, enter a description in the Say Something About This Photo box.

**10** To tag a person who appears in a given photo, click that photo's **Tag** button and then click that person's face and enter his or her name.

Continued

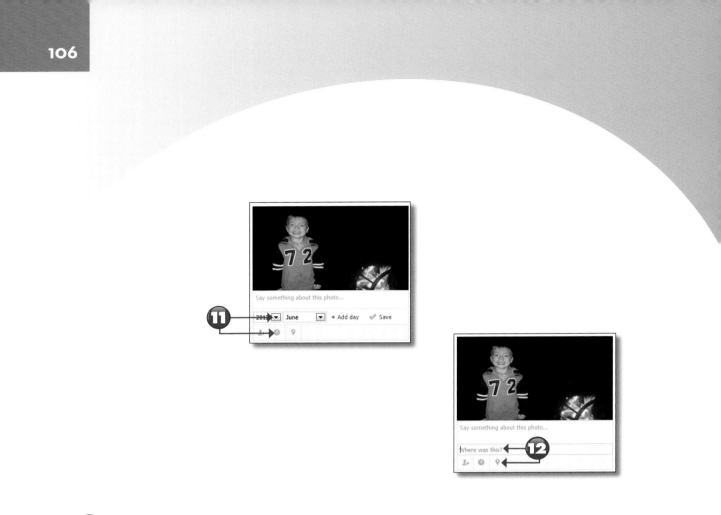

To enter the date a photo was taken, click that photo's **Date** button and then select the year, month, and date.

To enter the place a photo was taken, click that photo's **Location** button and then enter a location into the Where Was This? box.

Continued

**NOTE**

**Photos and Albums** The information you add to specific photos can be different from the information you enter for the album as a whole. ■

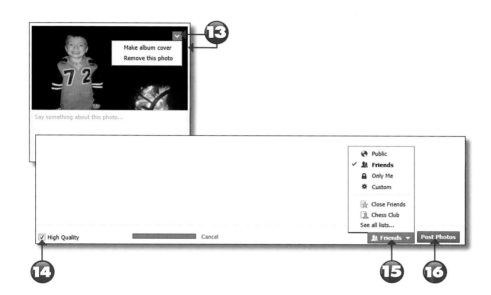

13 To select the image used as the cover photo for this album, click the **down arrow** on that photo and select **Make Album Cover**.

14 To upload photos in the highest possible resolution, check the **High Quality** option.

15 Click the **Privacy** button and select who can view the photos in this album: **Public**, **Friends**, **Only Me**, or **Custom**.

16 Click the **Post Photos** album when done.

*End*

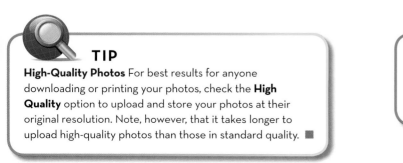

**TIP**

**High-Quality Photos** For best results for anyone downloading or printing your photos, check the **High Quality** option to upload and store your photos at their original resolution. Note, however, that it takes longer to upload high-quality photos than those in standard quality. ■

**NOTE**

**Album Cover** The album cover image is what others see when they view your albums on your Facebook Photos page. ■

# UPLOADING YOUR PICTURES TO AN EXISTING PHOTO ALBUM

After you've created a photo album, you can easily upload more photos to that album.

*Start*

1. Open your Facebook timeline page and click **Photos** to display your Photos page.

2. Click the album you want to add new photos to.

*Continued*

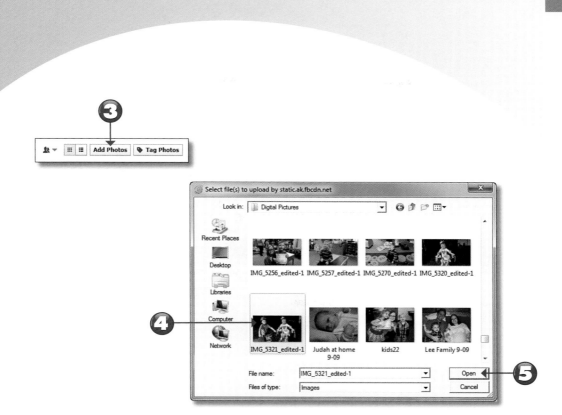

③ When the album page opens, click the **Add Photos** button.

④ When the Select Files to Upload dialog box appears, navigate to and select the photos to upload.

⑤ Click the **Open** button.

Continued

**TIP**

**Multiple Photos** You can add more than one photo at a time to an album. Hold down the **Ctrl** key while clicking files to select multiple files. ■

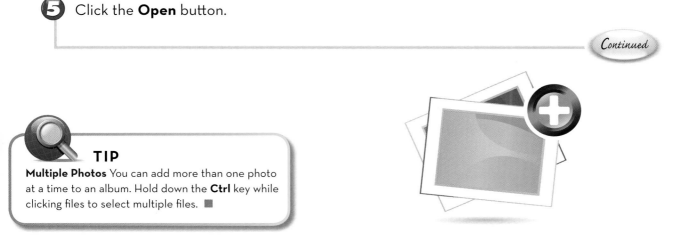

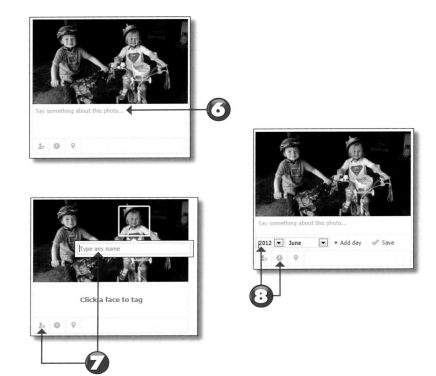

**6** The photos you selected are now added to the album page. To enter information about a specific picture, enter a description in the Say Something About This Photo box.

**7** To tag a person who appears in a given photo, click that photo's **Tag** button and then click that person's face and enter his or her name.

**8** To enter the date a photo was taken, click that photo's **Date** button and then select the year, month, and date.

Continued

**TIP**

**Location and Date** If the location and date of these photos are different from those already in the album, select a new location and date at the top of the album photos page. ■

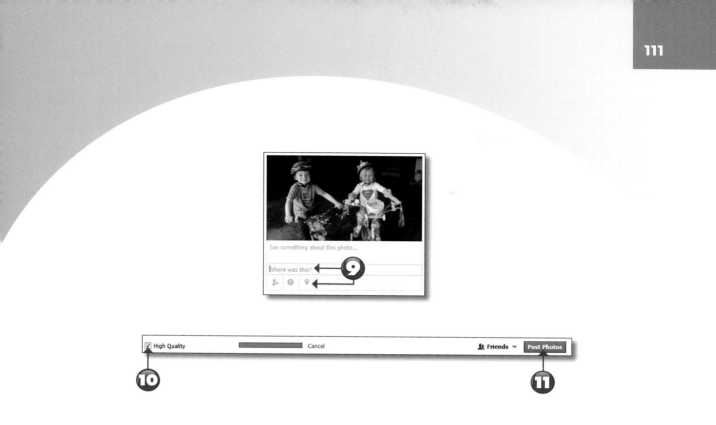

9 To enter the place a photo was taken, click that photo's **Location** button and then enter a location into the Where Was This? box.

10 To upload photos in the highest possible resolution, check the **High Quality** option.

11 Click the **Post Photos** button when done.

End

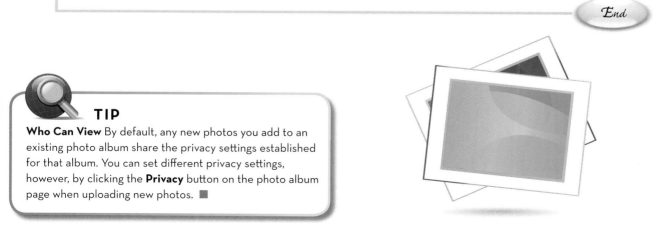

**TIP**

**Who Can View** By default, any new photos you add to an existing photo album share the privacy settings established for that album. You can set different privacy settings, however, by clicking the **Privacy** button on the photo album page when uploading new photos. ■

# TAGGING FRIENDS

You can, at any time, "tag" friends who appear in the photos you upload. This makes it easy for your friends to view themselves and other friends in your photos.

**Start**

1. Open the photo page for the picture you want to tag.

2. Click the **Tag Photo** button to the right of the photo.

Continued

## NOTE

**Multiple Tags** You can tag multiple people in each photo. For example, if you have a photo of you and your Uncle Vinnie, you can tag both yourself and Vinnie in the photo. This photo appears in your own photo albums, of course, but it also shows up on Vinnie's Photos page, in the Photos and Videos of Vinnie section. ■

## NOTE

**Where Tags Appear** When you tag a Facebook friend in a photo, a status update announcing that tag is placed in the friend's news feed, and the photo appears among the friend's Facebook photos (in the Photos and Videos of Friend section of the Photos page). ■

**3** In the photo, click the face of the person you want to tag.

**4** Facebook now displays a box around the selected person, along with a list of suggested friends. If the person's name is in this list, proceed to step 5. Otherwise, begin typing the name of the person into the text box.

**5** Click the person's name in the list.

**6** Click **Done Tagging**.

End

**NOTE**

**Face Recognition** Facebook employs face-recognition technology that attempts to automatically figure out which friends are in your pictures; if Facebook recognizes a face, it will suggest a friend's name for tagging. The goal is to make tagging pictures easier so that more people do it. ■

**NOTE**

**Non-Facebook Faces** If you enter the name of a person who isn't a Facebook member, Facebook prompts you to enter that person's email address. Facebook then emails that person a link to the photo and invites him to join Facebook and become your friend. ■

# EDITING A PHOTO'S DESCRIPTION

You can also, at any time, edit the description of a given photo.

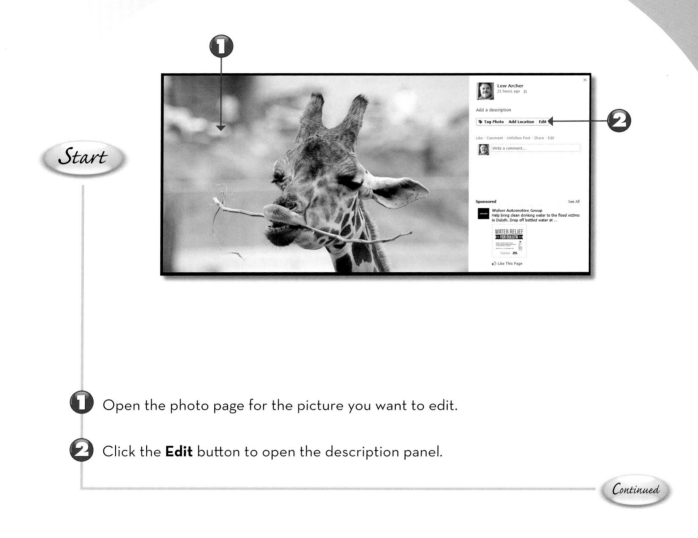

**Start**

**1** Open the photo page for the picture you want to edit.

**2** Click the **Edit** button to open the description panel.

Continued

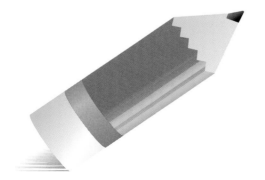

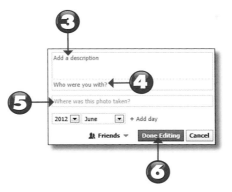

**3** Enter your description of the photo into the Add a Description box or edit the existing description.

**4** If you were with other people when the photo was taken, enter their names into the Who Were You With? box.

**5** To add locator information to the photo, enter where the photo was taken into the Where Was This Photo Taken? box.

**6** Click the **Done Editing** button.

*End*

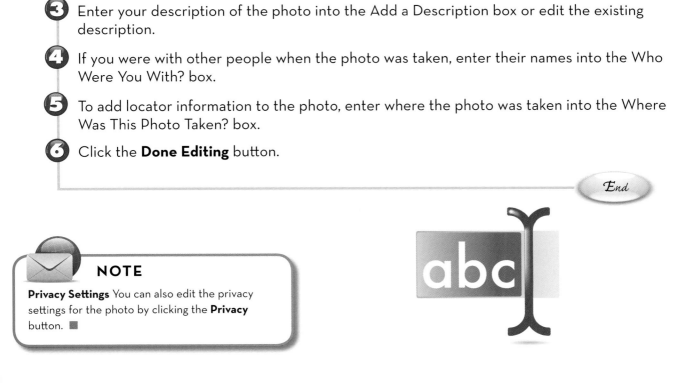

**NOTE**

**Privacy Settings** You can also edit the privacy settings for the photo by clicking the **Privacy** button. ■

# DELETING A PHOTO

If you later discover that you've uploaded a photo you don't want to share, Facebook lets you delete individual photos within an album.

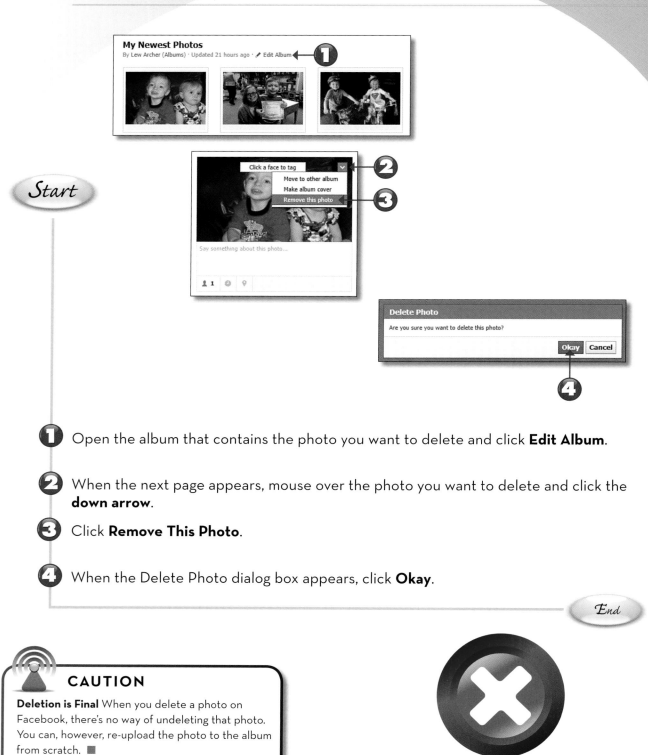

1. Open the album that contains the photo you want to delete and click **Edit Album**.

2. When the next page appears, mouse over the photo you want to delete and click the **down arrow**.

3. Click **Remove This Photo**.

4. When the Delete Photo dialog box appears, click **Okay**.

## CAUTION

**Deletion is Final** When you delete a photo on Facebook, there's no way of undeleting that photo. You can, however, re-upload the photo to the album from scratch. ■

# DELETING A PHOTO ALBUM

Facebook also lets you delete entire albums—and the photos contained within.

1. Open the album you want to delete and click **Edit Album**.

2. Click the **Delete Album** (trash can) button.

3. When the Delete Album dialog box appears, click the **Delete Album** button.

## CAUTION

**Delete All Photos** When you delete a photo album, you also delete all the photos within that album. ■

# EDITING A PHOTO ALBUM

You can, at any time, edit the title, description and other details of a photo album. You can change the location and date of the photos, as well as revise the privacy level.

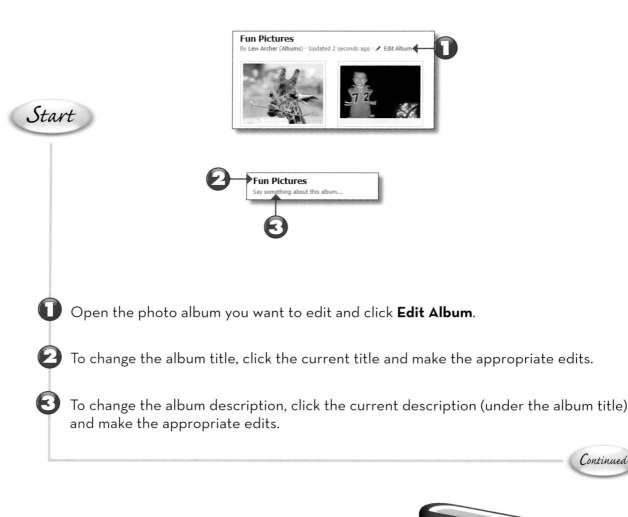

**1** Open the photo album you want to edit and click **Edit Album**.

**2** To change the album title, click the current title and make the appropriate edits.

**3** To change the album description, click the current description (under the album title) and make the appropriate edits.

Continued

## NOTE

**Album Info Versus Photo Info** The information (date, location, and so on) you add about an album applies to that album, not necessarily to the individual photos within the album. That is, information you add about a specific photo overrides the album information for that photo. ∎

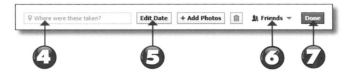

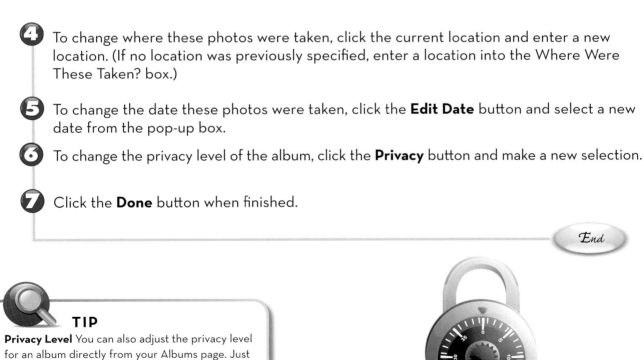

**4** To change where these photos were taken, click the current location and enter a new location. (If no location was previously specified, enter a location into the Where Were These Taken? box.)

**5** To change the date these photos were taken, click the **Edit Date** button and select a new date from the pop-up box.

**6** To change the privacy level of the album, click the **Privacy** button and make a new selection.

**7** Click the **Done** button when finished.

_End_

**TIP**

**Privacy Level** You can also adjust the privacy level for an album directly from your Albums page. Just click the **Privacy** button for a given album and make a selection from the pull-down menu. ■

# SHARING VIDEOS

In Chapter 8, "Sharing Pictures," you learned how to share your digital photos on Facebook. You can also share your home movies and other videos with friends and family on the Facebook site. As long as your videos are in digital format, it's easy to upload them to Facebook, where your Facebook friends can view them online.

That's not all. You can also share videos you find on the popular YouTube site with your Facebook friends. And not just your own videos, either; you can share any public YouTube video on your Facebook timeline.

# PLAYING A FACEBOOK VIDEO

Close video player

Person who
uploaded
video

Play previous
video

Play next
video

Comment on
video

Pause
video

Like video

Time slider

Share video

# VIEWING A FRIEND'S VIDEO

When one of your friends uploads a video to Facebook, it shows up in your news feed. You can play the video directly from the news feed or display the video in fullscreen mode.

**1** Navigate to the status update containing the video and click the video thumbnail to begin playback.

Continued

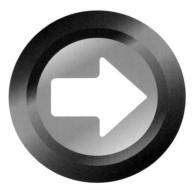

### TIP

**Sharing a Video** To share a friend's video with your friends via your timeline, click the **Share** link, and when the Share This video dialog box appears, enter your own text message before clicking the **Share Video** button. ■

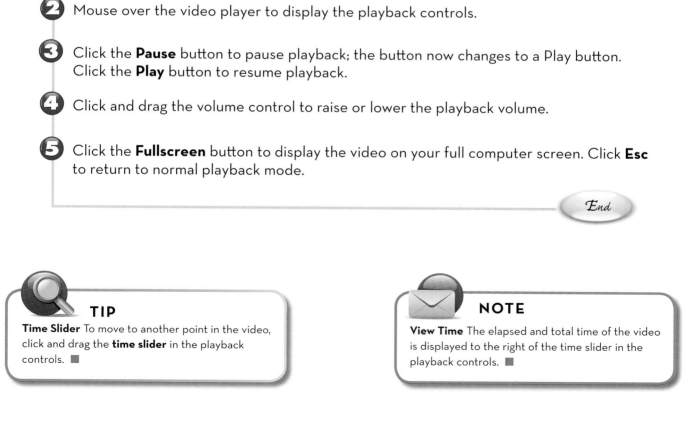

**2** Mouse over the video player to display the playback controls.

**3** Click the **Pause** button to pause playback; the button now changes to a Play button. Click the **Play** button to resume playback.

**4** Click and drag the volume control to raise or lower the playback volume.

**5** Click the **Fullscreen** button to display the video on your full computer screen. Click **Esc** to return to normal playback mode.

*End*

### TIP
**Time Slider** To move to another point in the video, click and drag the **time slider** in the playback controls. ■

### NOTE
**View Time** The elapsed and total time of the video is displayed to the right of the time slider in the playback controls. ■

# COMMENTING ON A FRIEND'S VIDEO

Just as you can comment on a friend's status update, you can also comment on any video he uploads. All comments are displayed beneath the video in the news feed.

Start

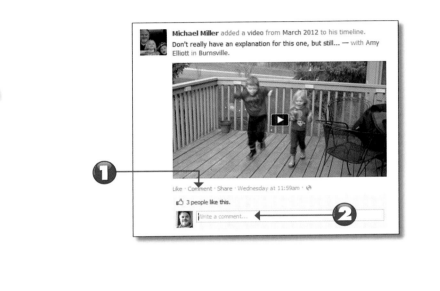

**1** Navigate to the video and click the **Comment** link beneath the thumbnail image. This expands the Write a Comment box.

**2** Type your comments into the Write a Comment box. Press **Enter** when done.

End

# LIKING A FRIEND'S VIDEO

If you like a friend's video, let him know by "liking" the video on Facebook.

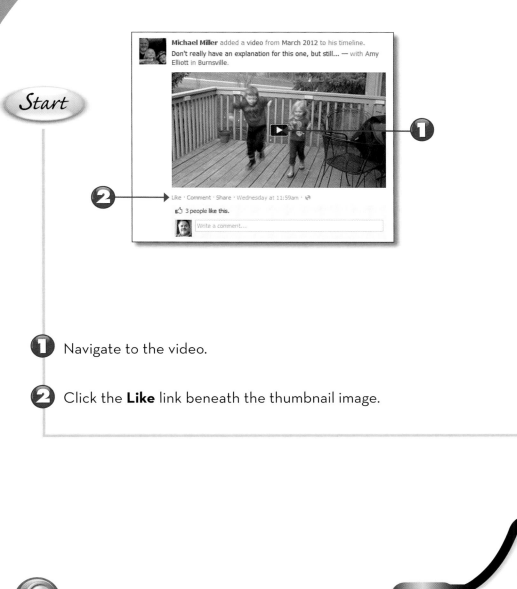

**Start**

**1** Navigate to the video.

**2** Click the **Like** link beneath the thumbnail image.

**End**

**TIP**

**Unlike a Video** If you later decide you don't like a given video, return to that video post and click the **Unlike** link. ▪

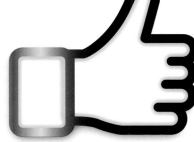

# VIEWING ALL OF A FRIEND'S VIDEOS

All the videos a friend has uploaded are displayed in a Videos album on the friend's Photos page. You can play back any video from there.

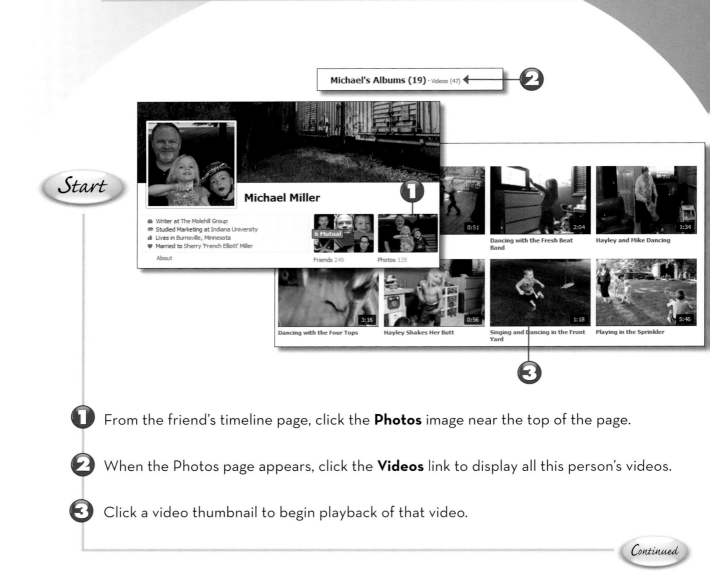

**①** From the friend's timeline page, click the **Photos** image near the top of the page.

**②** When the Photos page appears, click the **Videos** link to display all this person's videos.

**③** Click a video thumbnail to begin playback of that video.

*Continued*

**NOTE**

**Length** The video thumbnail images in the Videos album display the total length of each video. ■

**NOTE**

**Upload Order** The videos in the Videos album are organized by date uploaded; newest uploads are displayed first. ■

**4** Playback begins in a video player similar to Facebook's photo lightbox. To display playback controls, mouse over the video.

**5** To pause playback, click the **Pause** button. To resume playback, click the **Play** button.

**6** For those videos that were recorded and uploaded in high definition (HD), click the **HD** button to view the video in high def.

**7** To view the video fullscreen, click the **Fullscreen** button. Press **Esc** to return to the video playback page.

End

### TIP

**Like, Comment, and Share** To like a video from the individual video playback page, click **Like** in the description pane. To comment on the video, click **Comment**. To share the video on your own timeline, click **Share**. ■

### TIP

**Play Again** When the video is over, you can replay the video by clicking the **Play Again** button that appears in the video player window. ■

# UPLOADING YOUR OWN VIDEO

Facebook lets you upload just about any type of video and share it as a status update, which means all your friends should see it as part of their news feeds. Your uploaded videos also end up in the Videos album on your Photos page, accessible from your timeline for all your friends to view.

**1** Click your name on the Facebook toolbar to open your timeline page.

**2** Click the **Photos** image to open the Photos page.

**3** Click the **Add Videos** button to open the Create a New Video page.

*Continued*

## NOTE

**What to Upload** What kinds of videos can you upload to Facebook? Home movies are common, although you can upload other types of videos, so long as you're not uploading any copyrighted material. That means you can't upload commercial videos, videos that contain commercial music in the background, or videos with explicit material. ■

## TIP

**Upload Specs** Facebook lets you upload videos already stored as digital files, or create new videos in real-time from your computer's webcam. Videos must be no more than 20 minutes long, and no more than 1024MB in size. Facebook accepts videos in all major video file formats, including high-definition videos. ■

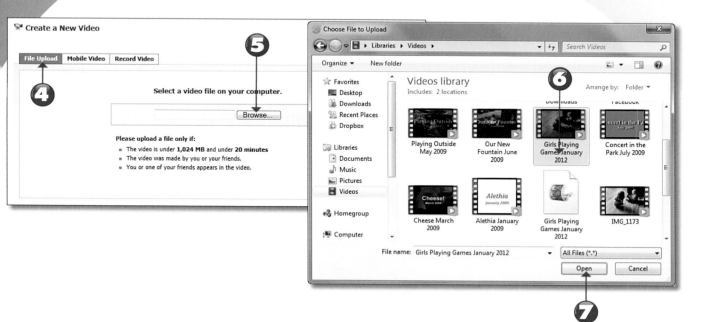

Click the **File Upload** tab.

Click the **Browse** button to display the Choose File to Upload dialog box.

Navigate to and select the video to upload.

Click the **Open** button.

Continued

**TIP**

**Video Resolution** When it comes to viewing videos, higher resolution is always better; the higher the resolution, the more detail in the picture. The best picture quality comes from so-called high-definition videos, which have the highest possible resolution. Facebook lets you upload videos at any resolution, so shoot, edit, and upload your videos in the highest resolution possible. ■

**TIP**

**Editing Videos** To edit the videos you take with a camcorder, you need a video-editing software program. The most popular programs include Adobe Premiere Elements (www.adobe.com/products/premiereel/, $99.99), Pinnacle Studio HD (www.pinnaclesys.com, $49.99), and Sony Vegas Movie Studio HD (www.sonycreativesoftware.com/moviestudiohd/, $49.95). ■

| File Upload | Mobile Video | Record Video | Back to My Videos |

**Please wait while your video is uploading.**

[ Cancel ]

**Enter the following info while you wait for your upload to finish.**

**8** Title:

**10** Where: Where was this video taken?

**9** Description:

Privacy: 👥 Friends ▼

[ Save Info ]

**8** You're now returned to the Create a New Video page, expanded. Enter a title for this video into the Title box.

**9** Enter a short description of the video into the Description box.

**10** To specify where the video was taken, enter a location into the Where box.

*Continued*

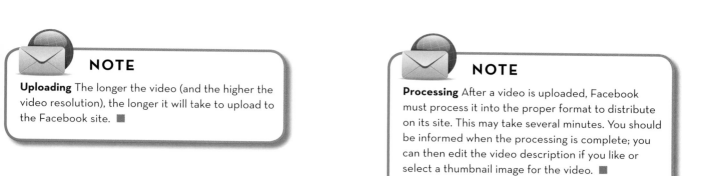

| File Upload | Mobile Video | Record Video | | Back to My Videos |

**Please wait while your video is uploading.**

[Cancel]

**Enter the following info while you wait for your upload to finish.**

Title: My Favorite Girls

Where: La Jolla Cove, Ca ×

Description: A short video of my two granddaughters.

Privacy: 👥 Friends ▾ ← **11**

**12** → Save Info

**11** Click the **Privacy** button and select who can view this video: **Public**, **Friends**, or **Custom**, as well as any friends lists you've created.

**12** Click the **Save Info** button when done.

*End*

**NOTE**

**Uploading** The longer the video (and the higher the video resolution), the longer it will take to upload to the Facebook site. ■

**NOTE**

**Processing** After a video is uploaded, Facebook must process it into the proper format to distribute on its site. This may take several minutes. You should be informed when the processing is complete; you can then edit the video description if you like or select a thumbnail image for the video. ■

# RECORDING A WEBCAM VIDEO

You can also upload videos recorded from your computer's webcam in real time. This is a great way to do a quick–and-dirty video for your Facebook friends, with no expensive camcorder or video-editing software required.

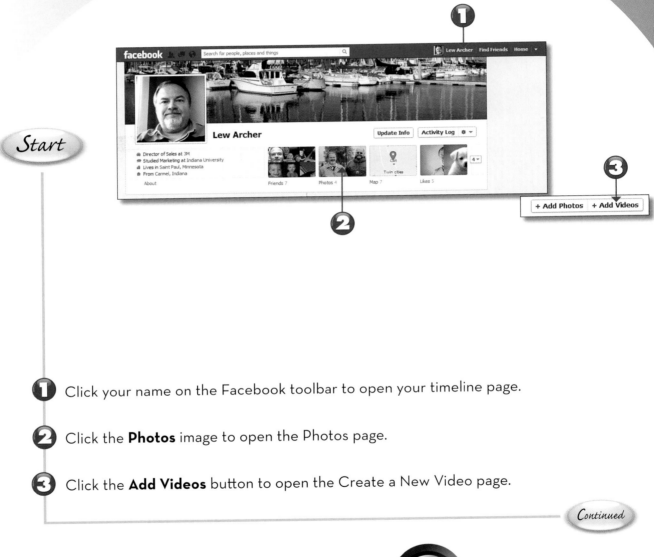

Start

1 Click your name on the Facebook toolbar to open your timeline page.

2 Click the **Photos** image to open the Photos page.

3 Click the **Add Videos** button to open the Create a New Video page.

Continued

## TIP

**Shooting Better Webcam Videos** One of the biggest problems with webcam videos is lack of light. You can improve the image quality by shining some sort of light on you, the subject. Aiming a desk lamp at your face, from in front, should do the job. ■

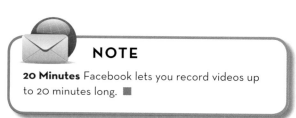

**4** Click the **Record Video** tab. You should now see a live shot from your computer's webcam.

**5** Click the red **Record** button to begin recording.

**6** When you're done recording, click the **Stop** button.

*Continued*

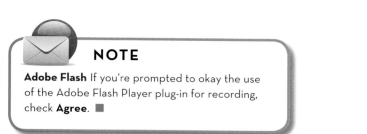

**NOTE**

**Adobe Flash** If you're prompted to okay the use of the Adobe Flash Player plug-in for recording, check **Agree**. ▪

**NOTE**

**20 Minutes** Facebook lets you record videos up to 20 minutes long. ▪

**7** To watch the video you just recorded, click the **Play** button.

**8** If you don't like what you see, click the **Reset** button to start over.

**9** To save the video you just recorded, click the **Save** button.

Continued

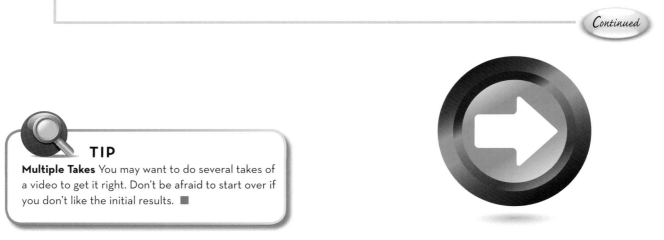

**TIP**

**Multiple Takes** You may want to do several takes of a video to get it right. Don't be afraid to start over if you don't like the initial results. ■

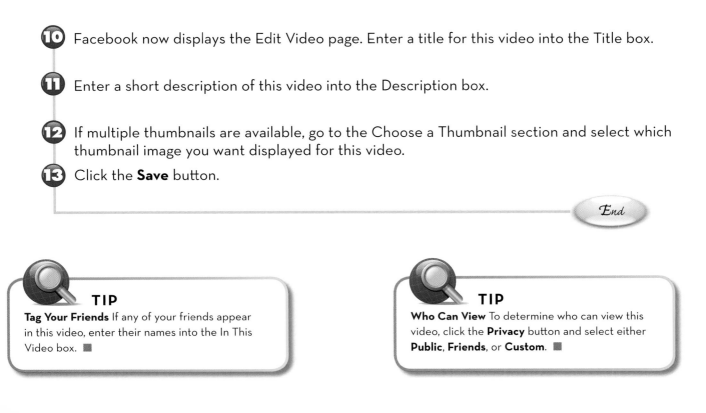

**10** Facebook now displays the Edit Video page. Enter a title for this video into the Title box.

**11** Enter a short description of this video into the Description box.

**12** If multiple thumbnails are available, go to the Choose a Thumbnail section and select which thumbnail image you want displayed for this video.

**13** Click the **Save** button.

*End*

**TIP**

**Tag Your Friends** If any of your friends appear in this video, enter their names into the In This Video box. ■

**TIP**

**Who Can View** To determine who can view this video, click the **Privacy** button and select either **Public**, **Friends**, or **Custom**. ■

# EDITING VIDEO INFORMATION

You can enter or edit information about any video you've uploaded at any time. You can also tag friends appearing in a video and select a thumbnail image to represent the video.

**Start**

① Click your name on the Facebook toolbar to open your timeline page.

② Click the **Photos** image to open the Photos page.

③ Click the **Videos** link to display all the videos you've uploaded.

④ Click the video you want to edit.

*Continued*

**NOTE**

**Editing** You can edit a video's title, location, date, description, tags, thumbnail image, and privacy level. ■

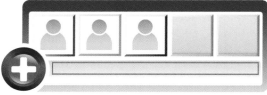

**5** When the video playback page appears, click the **Edit** link.

**6** To tag a person appearing in this video, enter his or her name into the In This Video box.

**7** To select a thumbnail image for this video, click the **left** and **right arrows** to cycle through ten preselected images.

**8** Make any additional changes and then click the **Save** button.

*End*

**TIP**

**Deleting a Video** To delete a video, open the video-editing page and click the **Delete** button.

# POSTING VIDEOS FROM YOUTUBE

Many Facebook users like to share videos from the YouTube site with their Facebook friends. You can share videos you've uploaded yourself or any public video from other YouTube users.

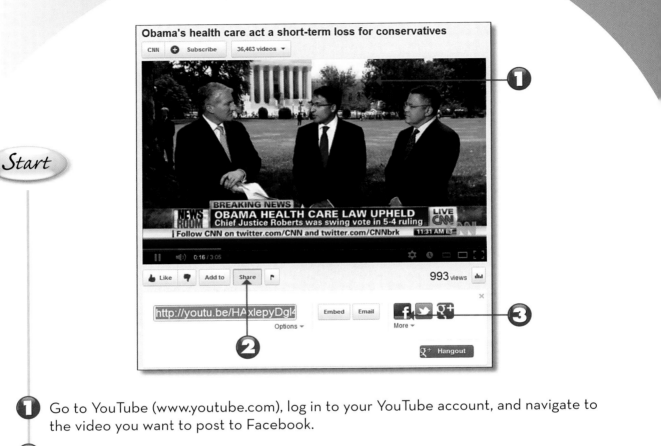

1. Go to YouTube (www.youtube.com), log in to your YouTube account, and navigate to the video you want to post to Facebook.

2. Click the **Share** button beneath the video player to expand the Share panel.

3. Click the **Facebook** button.

Continued

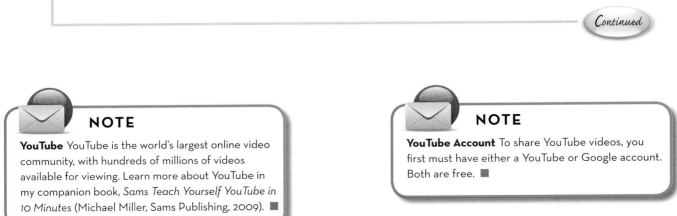

**NOTE**

**YouTube** YouTube is the world's largest online video community, with hundreds of millions of videos available for viewing. Learn more about YouTube in my companion book, *Sams Teach Yourself YouTube in 10 Minutes* (Michael Miller, Sams Publishing, 2009). ■

**NOTE**

**YouTube Account** To share YouTube videos, you first must have either a YouTube or Google account. Both are free. ■

**4** When the Share This Link window appears, enter an accompanying message into the Write Something box.

**5** Select a thumbnail to display (if more than one thumbnail image is available), or check the **No Thumbnail** option to post the video without a corresponding thumbnail image.

**6** Click the **Share Link** button. The video is now posted as a status update to your Facebook timeline.

*End*

### NOTE

**Linking Accounts** The first time you try to share a YouTube video on Facebook, you see the Facebook Login window. Enter your email address and Facebook password and then click the **Login** button. (You won't see this window after this first time.) ■

### TIP

**Larger Files** Because YouTube video files can be twice as large (2GB) as those allowed for direct uploading to Facebook, embedding a YouTube video might be a better way to share larger video files, such as those recorded in high definition. ■

# TEXT AND VIDEO CHATTING

Not all communication has to be shared publicly. Facebook also lets you communicate privately with your friends online, via a private message system and via real-time chat sessions.

In fact, you can engage in either text or video chat. Video chat is especially nice if both you and your friend are connected at the same time and have webcams on your computers. It's just like being there!

# TEXT CHATTING

Click to change
to video chat

Click to configure
chat options

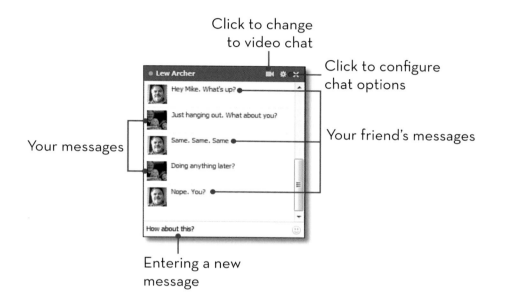

Your messages

Your friend's messages

Entering a new
message

# SENDING A PRIVATE MESSAGE

Facebook lets any user send private messages to any other user. These messages do not appear in anyone's news feed or timeline; it's the Facebook equivalent of email.

**1** From your Facebook home page, go to the Favorites section of the navigation pane and click **Messages**.

**2** This displays the Messages page; click the **New Message** button.

*Continued*

**NOTE**

**Facebook Email** One important feature of Facebook's Messages system is that every Facebook member now has a @facebook.com email address, linked to his or her Facebook username and account. To claim your email address, go to the Messages page and click the **Claim Your Facebook Email** link. ■

**NOTE**

**Email or Private Message** When you send a message to another Facebook user, it's delivered via Facebook's private message system. When you send a message to someone who is not a Facebook user, it's delivered via email, using your Facebook email address. ■

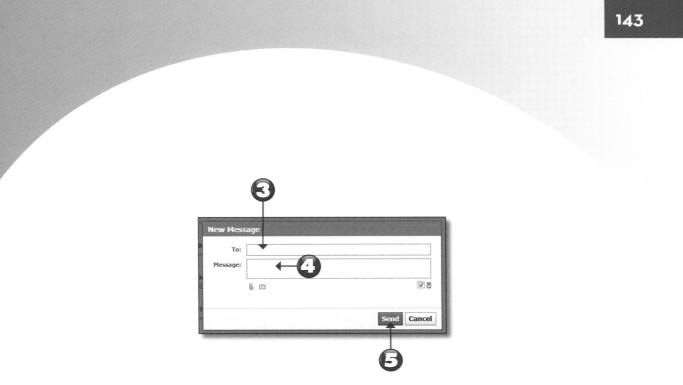

**3** When the New Message dialog box appears, enter the name of the recipient into the To box.

**4** Enter your message into the Message box.

**5** Press **Enter** or click the **Send** button to send the message on its way.

*End*

**TIP**

**Attaching a File** You can use Facebook's private message system to send files to other users. When creating a new message, click the **paperclip** icon to open the Open dialog box; navigate to and select the file you want to attach and then click the **Open** button. ▪

**TIP**

**Sharing a Photo** To attach a picture or video to a new private message, click the **Camera** icon. This opens the Open dialog box; navigate to and select the file you want to attach and then click the **Open** button. ▪

# VIEWING YOUR MESSAGES

New messages are displayed when you click the **Messages** button on the Facebook toolbar. You can view all your private messages from the Messages page.

---

**1** From your Facebook home page, go to the Favorites section of the navigation pane and click **Messages** to display the Messages page.

**2** All your messages and communications you've received are displayed here, newest first. Click a message header to read the message.

*Continued*

---

### NOTE

**All Messages** The Messages page consolidates all messages received from across the Facebook site, including email messages, private messages, chat messages, and text messages sent via mobile phone. ■

### TIP

**Conversations** Because Messages sorts all communications by user, you create an ongoing archive of all your conversations with each of your friends. It's a lifelong conversational history, so you always know what you've talked about. ■

**3** The resulting page lists all messages to and from that person in the form of a flowing conversation; newest messages are at the bottom of the page.

**4** To send another message to this person, simply enter your message into the text box at the bottom of the page and click **Reply** or press **Enter**.

*End*

### TIP

**Different Types of Messages** The type of message is indicated by an icon on the far right side of the message list, beside the time/date indicator. An envelope icon indicates an email message; a word balloon icon indicates a chat or instant message; a phone icon indicates a text message; and no icon means you got a private message from a Facebook friend. ■

### NOTE

**Other Messages** Not all messages are displayed on the main Messages page; you only see messages from Facebook members, not messages sent via email from outsiders. Click **Other** in the Messages section of the sidebar to display email messages sent from non-Facebook members, as well as messages and invitations from pages to which you've subscribed. ■

# STARTING A CHAT SESSION

Facebook chat is a form of online instant messaging; it's kind of like text messaging, but on your computer instead of your phone. You can carry on real-time text conversations with any of your friends who are also online and willing to talk.

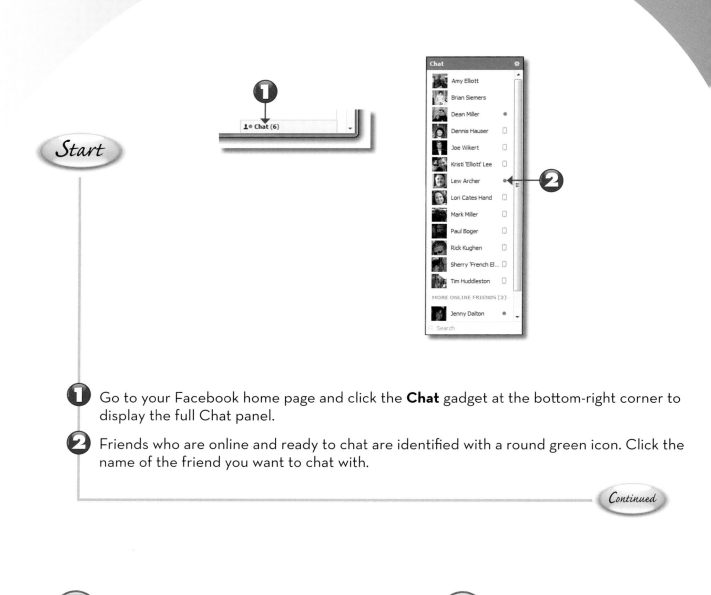

*Start*

1 Go to your Facebook home page and click the **Chat** gadget at the bottom-right corner to display the full Chat panel.

2 Friends who are online and ready to chat are identified with a round green icon. Click the name of the friend you want to chat with.

*Continued*

**NOTE**

**Friends on Chat** There's also a Friends on Chat section at the bottom of the navigation pane. Unfortunately, this section does not display *everyone* who's available to chat. The Chat panel is a better place to find friends currently online. ■

**NOTE**

**Chat Sidebar** If your web browser is displayed wide enough onscreen, you see a persistent Chat sidebar on the far right side of your Facebook home page instead of the pop-up Chat list. ■

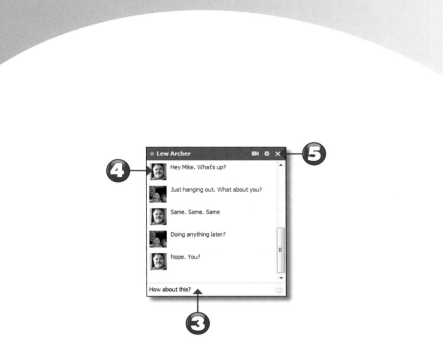

This opens a chat panel with the selected friend. Type a text message in the bottom text box and press **Enter**.

Your messages, along with your friend's responses, appear in consecutive order within the Chat panel. Continue typing new messages as you want.

To end the chat session and close the Chat panel, click the X at the top right of the panel.

End

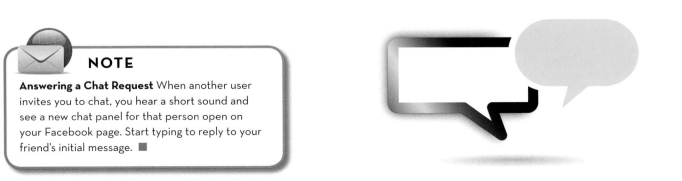

### NOTE

**Answering a Chat Request** When another user invites you to chat, you hear a short sound and see a new chat panel for that person open on your Facebook page. Start typing to reply to your friend's initial message. ■

# LAUNCHING A VIDEO CHAT

If you have a webcam installed on your computer, you can talk to other Facebook users face to face, with Facebook's video chat feature. Naturally, the friend you want to talk to also has to have a webcam on her PC and be online at the same time you are.

**1** Go to your friend's timeline page and click the **Call** button.

*Continued*

**NOTE**

**Skype** Facebook's video chat feature is powered by Skype, one of the more popular Internet-based voice and video communication services. ■

**NOTE**

**Install the Chat Applet** The first time you use Facebook's video chat, you'll be are prompted to download and install the necessary background chat applet on your computer. Follow the onscreen instructions to do so. ■

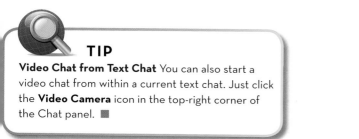

**2** When your friend answers the call, Facebook displays the video chat window. Your friend appears in the main part of the window; your picture is in a smaller window at the top right. All you have to do is talk.

**3** When you're ready to close the chat, hover over the chat window and then click the **X** at the top-right corner.

*End*

**TIP**

**Video Chat from Text Chat** You can also start a video chat from within a current text chat. Just click the **Video Camera** icon in the top-right corner of the Chat panel. ■

**TIP**

**Video Messages** If your friend is unavailable to chat, Facebook prompts you to leave a video message for that person. Your friend can then view and respond to that message when she's next online. ■

## Chapter 11

# WORKING WITH FACEBOOK PAGES, APPS, AND GAMES

Facebook is about more than sharing with your friends. You can also sign up as a "fan" of celebrities and companies you like and let them share their latest news with you. It's a great way to participate in a community of people who share similar interests.

You can also enhance Facebook with third-party apps. These are services and utilities that build on Facebook's community and sharing features to offer additional functionality to you and other users.

The most popular Facebook apps are actually games—social games, to be precise. You play some of these games by yourself and others with your Facebook friends. If nothing else, Facebook games are fun and help you waste a lot of time!

# FACEBOOK CELEBRITY AND COMPANY PAGES

Singer Adele's Facebook page

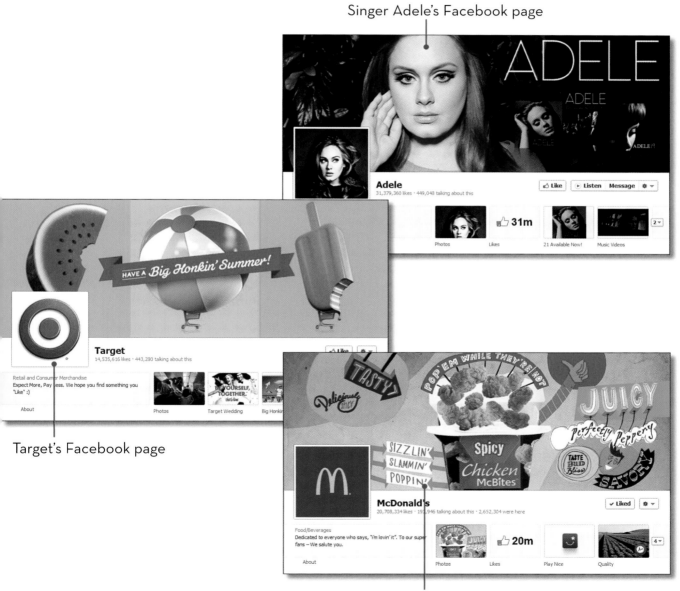

Target's Facebook page

McDonald's Facebook page

# LIKING A FACEBOOK PAGE

Even though businesses, celebrities, and public figures aren't regular users, they still want to use Facebook to connect with their customers and fans. They do this through Facebook pages—essentially timeline pages for companies and public figures. If you're a fan of a given company or celebrity, you can "like" that entity's Facebook page—and participate in that larger community.

Start

To find a specific page, enter one or more keywords that describe the person, company, or organization into the Search box on the Facebook toolbar and then click the **Search** button.

When the search results page appears, click the **Pages** link in the sidebar.

To view a specific page, click the page's name in the list.

Continued

**NOTE**

**Who Gets a Page?** Just about any public person or entity can create a Facebook page. You can create Facebook pages for businesses, brands, and products; for musicians, actors, and other celebrities; for politicians, public servants, and other public figures; and for school classes, public organizations, special events, and social causes. ■

**NOTE**

**Page Community** Most companies and celebrities with Facebook pages use their pages to keep their customers or fans informed of news and events. When you like a page, status updates from that person or company appear in your Facebook news feed. ■

4. Click an app to view that specific content.

5. To send a message to this person or company, enter the message into the Write Something box and then press **Enter**.

6. To become a fan of this page, click the **Like** button.

*End*

**NOTE**

**Navigating a Page** A Facebook fan page is very similar to a standard Facebook personal timeline page, right down to the timeline of updates and events. Pages can feature specialized apps, however, which are located at the top of the page, under the cover image. For example, a musician's page might feature an audio player app for that performer's songs. ■

**TIP**

**Creating Your Own Page** If you want to create your own page for your business or community organization, go to www.facebook.com/pages/, click the **Create Page** button, and follow the onscreen instructions from there. ■

# DISCOVERING APPS AND GAMES

A Facebook application (app) is simply a program or game that runs on the Facebook site. These apps are accessed from their own Facebook pages, and you use them while you're signed in to Facebook. Some apps build on the social networking nature of the Facebook site; others are designed for more solitary use. Some are strictly functional; others are more fun. There are a wide range of apps available—you're bound to find some that look interesting to you.

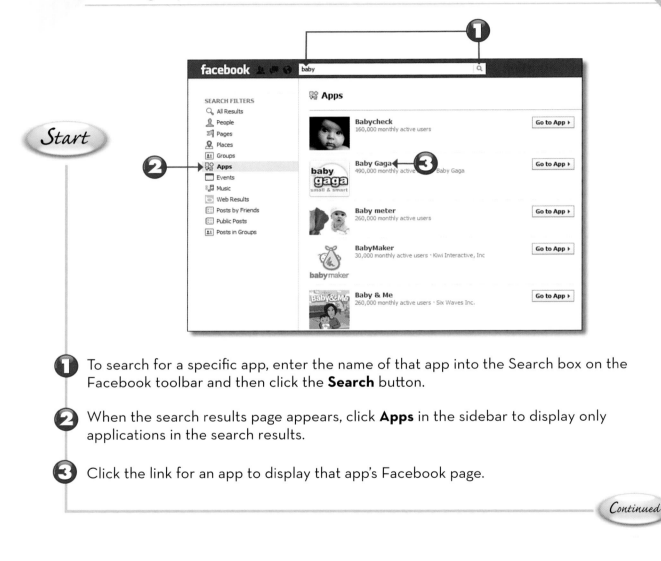

*Start*

**1** To search for a specific app, enter the name of that app into the Search box on the Facebook toolbar and then click the **Search** button.

**2** When the search results page appears, click **Apps** in the sidebar to display only applications in the search results.

**3** Click the link for an app to display that app's Facebook page.

*Continued*

---

**NOTE**

**Third-Party Apps** Although some applications are developed by Facebook, most are created by third-party application developers. The vast majority of Facebook applications, including third-party apps, are available free of charge. ■

**TIP**

**App Directory** To browse all available apps by category, visit the Facebook application directory, located at www.facebook.com/apps/. ■

 If you want to use that application or play that game, follow the onscreen instructions to proceed.

*End*

**NOTE**

**App Pages** The page for a Facebook app contains important information about that application—including, in many instances, reviews from users of that app. ■

**NOTE**

**Request for Permission** When you start using an app or game, you may be prompted with a Request for Permission to access your personal information on Facebook. Click the **Allow** button to proceed. ■

# VIEWING AND MANAGING YOUR APPS AND GAMES

Want to see and manage the applications you're using? There are probably a lot more than you might remember.

Start

① Go to the Apps section in the navigation section of your Facebook home page and click **More**.

② This displays the Apps page, with all your apps listed. Click any link to view the page for that application.

Continued

## TIP

**Favorite Apps** To add an app to the Favorites section on your Facebook home page, click the **Pencil** icon and select **Add to Favorites**. ■

**③** To edit the settings for a particular app, click the **Pencil** icon to the left of the app name and click **Edit Settings** from the pop-up menu.

**④** You now see an Edit Settings dialog box for that application. Make the desired changes and then click the **Close** button.

*End*

**NOTE**

**App Settings** Each app has different settings available in its Edit Settings dialog box. Some apps don't have any settings to configure. ■

**TIP**

**Deleting Apps** To delete an application you're no longer using, click the **Pencil** icon next to that app's name and select **Remove App**. When you're prompted to confirm the deletion, click the **Remove** button. ■

# SHARING EVENTS AND BIRTHDAYS

Facebook lets you share more than just status updates and photos. You can also share upcoming events—that is, create and announce events online and then invite specific Facebook friends. It's a great way to manage parties, meetings, and the like, all within the Facebook infrastructure.

The most common type of event is a birthday, and Facebook helps out there, too. Facebook will notify you of your friends' upcoming birthdays and make it easy for you to send your birthday greetings. Facebook will even announce your birthday to your friends—so sit back and wait for those well-wishes to arrive!

# VIEWING AN EVENT

Time and date of event

Definitely attending

Invited

Description

Location

Discussion about the event

# SEARCHING FOR EVENTS

When a friend invites you to an event, that invitation appears in your news feed and in the Events section at the top-right corner of your Facebook home page. You can also search Facebook for specific events—the better to find events in which you're interested.

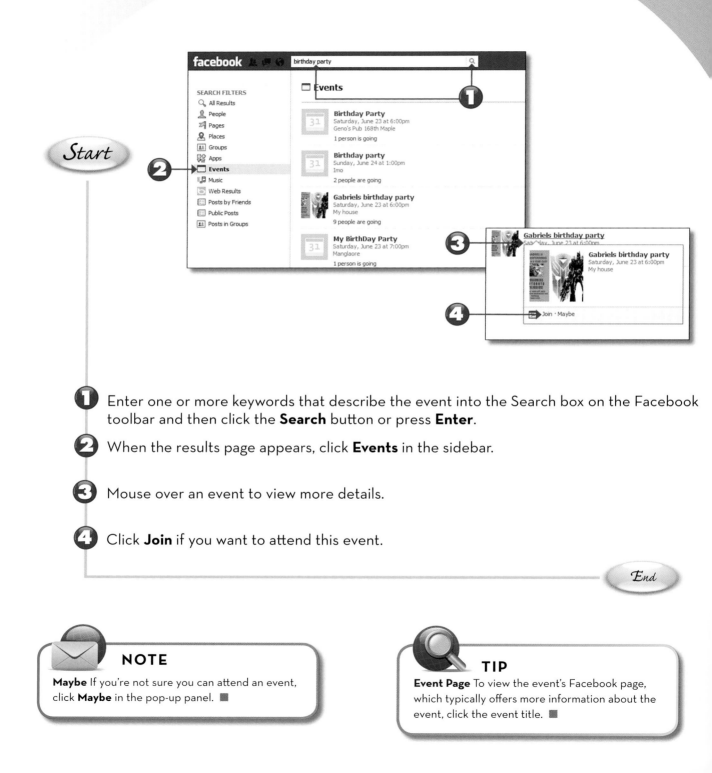

1. Enter one or more keywords that describe the event into the Search box on the Facebook toolbar and then click the **Search** button or press **Enter**.

2. When the results page appears, click **Events** in the sidebar.

3. Mouse over an event to view more details.

4. Click **Join** if you want to attend this event.

---

**NOTE**

**Maybe** If you're not sure you can attend an event, click **Maybe** in the pop-up panel. ■

**TIP**

**Event Page** To view the event's Facebook page, which typically offers more information about the event, click the event title. ■

# RESPONDING TO AN EVENT FROM A STATUS UPDATE

When you've been invited to an event, a status update to that effect appears in your Facebook news feed. You can respond to that invitation directly from your news feed.

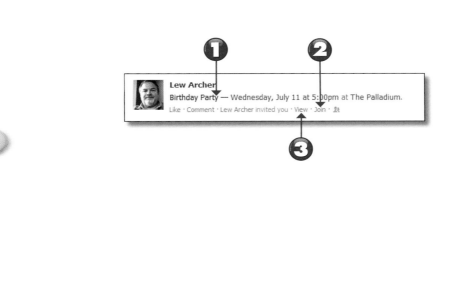

1 Scroll to the status update that contains the event invitation.

2 To accept the invitation, click **Join**.

3 To view more about the event, click **View**. This displays the full event page.

*End*

**NOTE**

**Joining** Accepting an event invitation is now called *joining* that event. In the past, Facebook called it RSVP'ing. ◼

**TIP**

**No Obligation** You should feel no obligation to accept any specific event. Only accept those you genuinely want to and can attend. ◼

# VIEWING THE EVENT PAGE

When you've been invited to an event, that invitation appears in the Notification menu on the Facebook toolbar. Events that you're invited to also appear in your news feed and on the dedicated Events page.

**1** Go to your Facebook home page and click **Events** in the navigation sidebar to display your Events page.

**2** Click the name of an event to view the page for that event.

Continued

**TIP**

**Liking and Commenting** You can like and comment on an event invitation the same as you do with any status update. Just click the **Like** or **Comment** link underneath the status update for that event invitation. ■

**TIP**

**Suggested Events** To view events that Facebook thinks you might like to attend, click **Suggested Events** in the navigation sidebar. ■

**③** The event page contains much useful information about the event. To accept the invitation, click the **Join** button.

**④** To tell the host that you might attend the event, click the **Maybe** button.

**⑤** To tell the host that you won't be coming, click the **Decline** button.

*End*

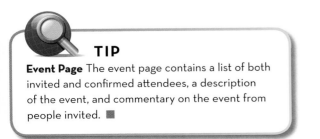

**TIP**

**Event Page** The event page contains a list of both invited and confirmed attendees, a description of the event, and commentary on the event from people invited. ◼

# CREATING A NEW EVENT

Facebook lets you create all manner of events, from parties to community meetings, and invite selected friends to those events. You can then manage that event through the event's Facebook page.

**Start**

**1** From your Facebook home page, click **Events** in the navigation sidebar to display your Events page.

**2** Click the **Create Event** button.

Continued

> **NOTE**
>
> **Public or Private** You can create events that are visible to the general public, visible to your friends list only, or visible only to those individuals invited to the event. ■

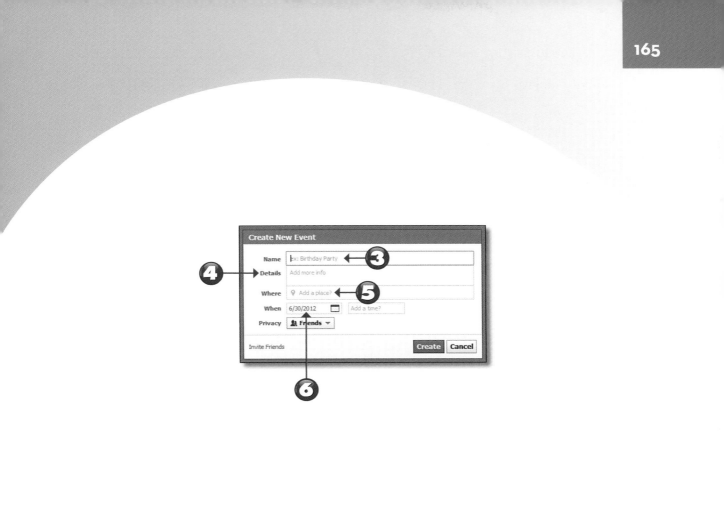

**3** When the Create Event dialog box appears, enter the name of the event into the Name box.

**4** Enter any additional details about the event into the Details box.

**5** To specify the event's location, enter the location into the Where box.

**6** Enter the date of the event into the When section.

Continued

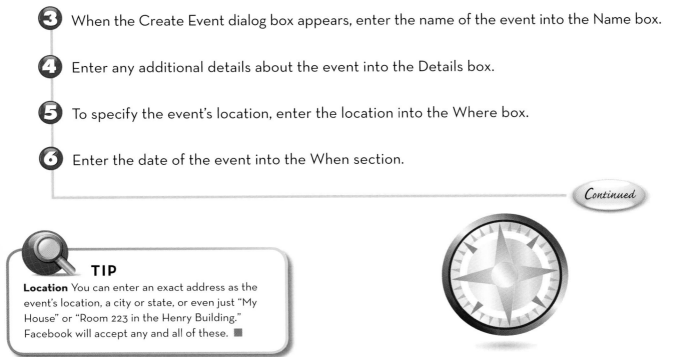

**TIP**

**Location** You can enter an exact address as the event's location, a city or state, or even just "My House" or "Room 223 in the Henry Building." Facebook will accept any and all of these. ■

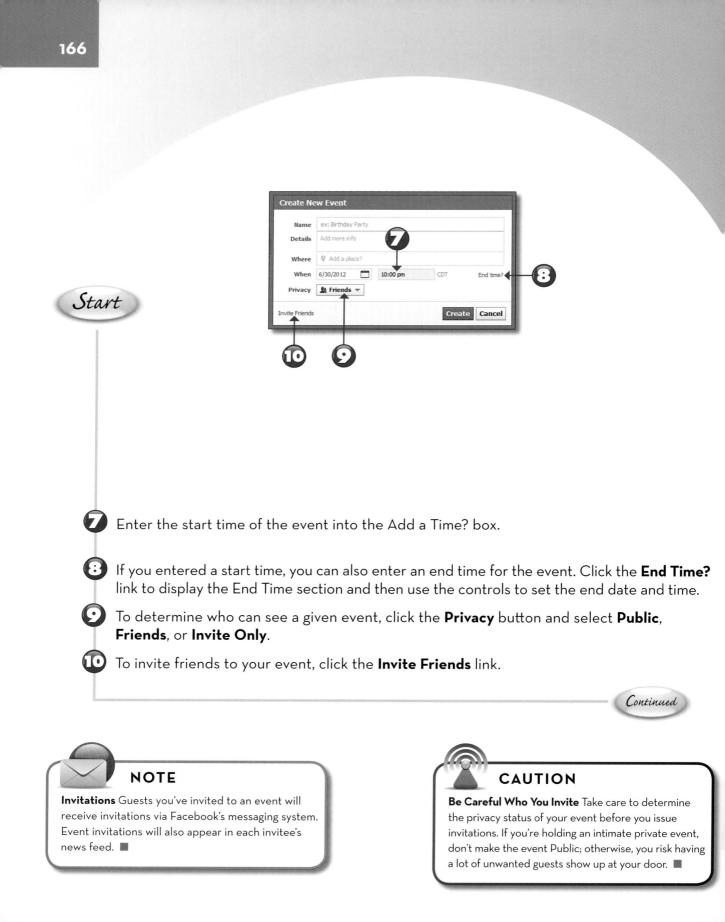

**Start**

**7** Enter the start time of the event into the Add a Time? box.

**8** If you entered a start time, you can also enter an end time for the event. Click the **End Time?** link to display the End Time section and then use the controls to set the end date and time.

**9** To determine who can see a given event, click the **Privacy** button and select **Public**, **Friends**, or **Invite Only**.

**10** To invite friends to your event, click the **Invite Friends** link.

Continued

## NOTE

**Invitations** Guests you've invited to an event will receive invitations via Facebook's messaging system. Event invitations will also appear in each invitee's news feed. ■

## CAUTION

**Be Careful Who You Invite** Take care to determine the privacy status of your event before you issue invitations. If you're holding an intimate private event, don't make the event Public; otherwise, you risk having a lot of unwanted guests show up at your door. ■

**11** When the Invite Friends dialog box appears, check those friends you want to invite.

**12** Click the **Save** button.

**13** When you're returned to the Create New Event dialog box, click the **Create** button to create the event and send out the desired invitations.

*End*

**TIP**

**Viewing Your Events** To view the events you've created, click the **Events** link in the navigation sidebar of your Facebook home page. Your Events page lists both events you've created and have been invited to. ■

**TIP**

**Editing an Event** To edit an event you've created, click the **Events** link in the home page navigation sidebar and then click the event in question. When the event page appears, click the **Edit** button and have at it. ■

# CELEBRATING FRIENDS' BIRTHDAYS

Facebook knows a lot about you and your friends, including when you were born. To that end, Facebook does a nice social service by letting you know when someone's birthday is approaching—so that you can prepare your birthday wishes.

*Start*

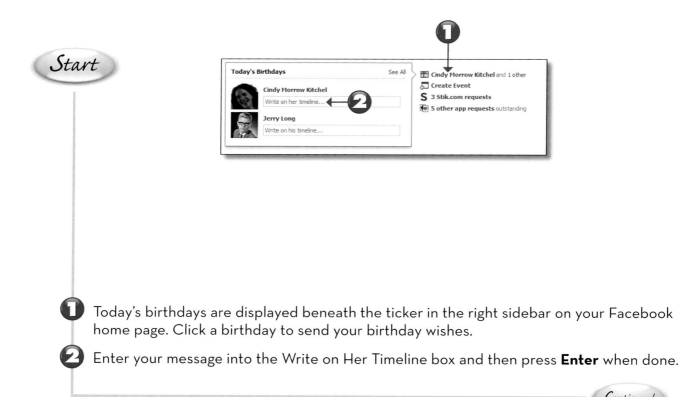

**1** Today's birthdays are displayed beneath the ticker in the right sidebar on your Facebook home page. Click a birthday to send your birthday wishes.

**2** Enter your message into the Write on Her Timeline box and then press **Enter** when done.

*Continued*

### NOTE

**Public Only** Facebook will only notify you of birthdays from friends who have opted to make their birthdate public. Friends with private birthdays will not appear in the birthday list. ■

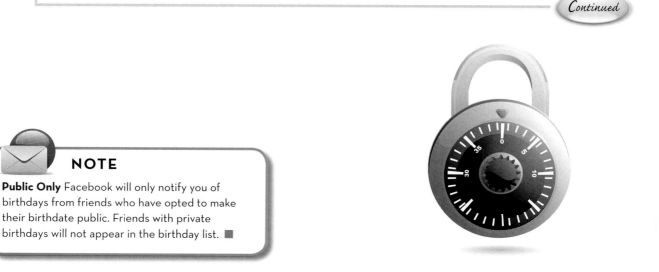

**3** To view all upcoming birthdays, click **Events** in the home page navigation sidebar to display the Events page.

**4** Scroll to a specific birthday section and click a name to view that individual's timeline page.

**5** Enter your personal message into the Write Something box and then press **Enter** to post that message to your friend's timeline.

*End*

### NOTE

**Personal Replies** Most people receive a ton of Facebook greetings on their birthdays. Don't be disappointed if you don't receive a personal thank you from the birthday baby. ■

Chapter 13

# KEEPING PRIVATE THINGS PRIVATE

Facebook is a social network, and being social means sharing one's personal information with others. In Facebook's case, you share your information by default—both with your friends and with Facebook and its partners and advertisers.

Unfortunately, all this sharing poses a problem if you'd rather keep some things private. If you share everything with everyone, then all sorts of information can get out—and be seen by people you don't want seeing it. Keeping personal information personal on Facebook is possible, but it requires some work on your part.

# FACEBOOK PRIVACY SETTINGS

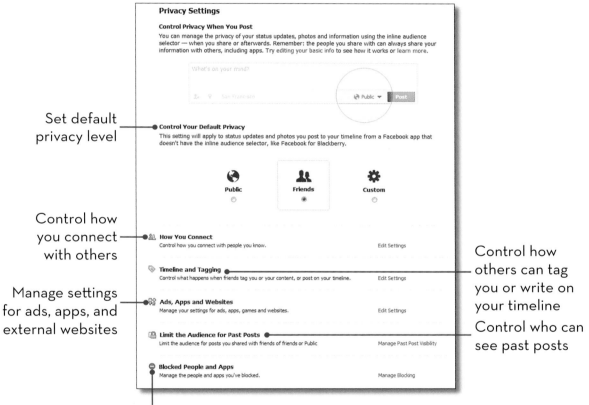

Set default privacy level

Control how you connect with others

Manage settings for ads, apps, and external websites

Control how others can tag you or write on your timeline

Control who can see past posts

Manage blocked people and apps

# WHAT *NOT* TO POST ON FACEBOOK

It might be difficult to tell from reading some people's overly personal posts, but there are some bits of information you probably shouldn't post on Facebook for the entire world to see. You should always remember that Facebook is *not* a private diary; it's a public website with more than 800 million users. Some things simply shouldn't be shared with all those users.

*Start*

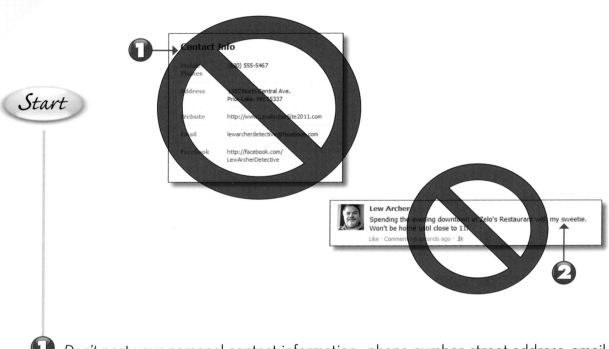

**1** *Don't* post your personal contact information—phone number, street address, email address, and so forth. You don't want complete strangers to contact or harass you.

**2** *Don't* post location information when you're away from home. This can tip off burglars that your house is empty or notify stalkers where you can be found.

*Continued*

 **CAUTION**

**Don't Accept Every Friend Request** You don't need to have a thousand friends. It's better to have a smaller number of true friends than a larger number of people you really don't know. ■

**CAUTION**

**They May Not Even Be Real, Let Alone Friends** When you have hundreds of people on your Facebook friends list, how well do you really know any of them? It's possible that some of the people you call "friends" really aren't the people they present themselves to be. For whatever reason, some people adopt different personas—including fake names and profile pictures—when they're online. It's possible that you're establishing relationships on these social networks that have no basis in reality. ■

**3** Don't criticize your employer or teacher in status updates. They can read your posts just like anyone else can.

**4** Don't get overly political or controversial in your posts. This can turn off potential employers or even old friends.

*Continued*

 **CAUTION**

**Play It Safe** You shouldn't post anything on Facebook that could possibly be used against you by a teacher, co-worker, employer, police agency, or even a vengeful ex-spouse. When you post a status update, it's there for everyone to see—friend or foe. ■

 **CAUTION**

**Don't Gripe** The last thing your Facebook friends want to find in their news feeds is your private griping. It's okay to grouse and be grumpy from time to time, but don't use Facebook as your personal forum for petty grievances. If you have a personal problem, deal with it; whining gets old really fast. ■

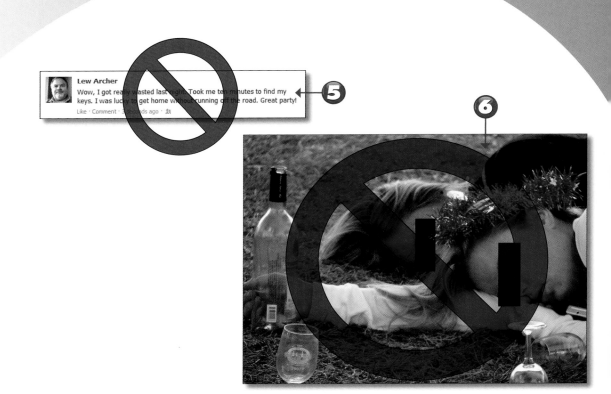

**5** Don't post information about embarrassing behavior, such as getting drunk at a party. Potential employers might read this and think twice about hiring you.

**6** Don't post embarrassing photos or tag others in embarrassing photos. You don't need public photographic proof of your indiscretions.

Continued

**CAUTION**

**Be Discrete** Remember that by default, Facebook status updates are public for all to read. Post only that information that you'd want your friends (or spouse or employer or children) to read. ■

**CAUTION**

**Don't Assume Everyone Agrees with You** Some people like to use Facebook as a platform for their opinions. While it might be okay to share your opinions with close real-world friends, spouting off in a public forum is not only bad form, it's a way to incite a flame war—an unnecessary online war of words. ■

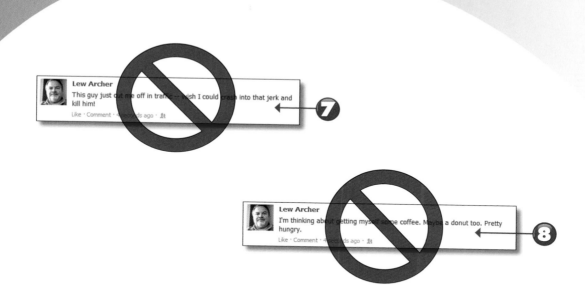

**7** Don't post without thinking first. It's difficult to take back something once it's been posted.

**8** Don't post if you don't have anything interesting to say. Posting too many meaningless updates will cause friends to defriend you.

*End*

## CAUTION

**It's Not a Dating Service** You might meet new friends on Facebook, but use caution about transferring online friendships into the physical world. You should never arrange to meet privately with an online "friend" with whom you've never met in person; he may turn out to be a predator. If you must meet an online friend in person, take someone else with you and meet in a public place. ■

## CAUTION

**You're Not Invisible** You need to remember that on Facebook, you're not invisible. Facebook is a public community; everything you post might be readable by anyone. Post only information that is safe enough for your family, friends, and co-workers to read. ■

# CONTROLLING DEFAULT PRIVACY SETTINGS

Facebook likes to share all your information with just about everybody on its social network—including advertisers and third-party websites. Fortunately, you can configure Facebook to be much less public than it is by default. You can opt to share your information with everyone on Facebook, just your friends, or with a custom subset of friends.

Start

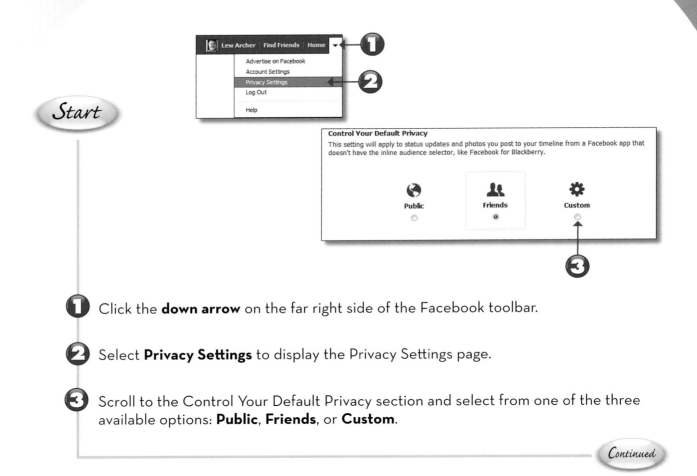

1 Click the **down arrow** on the far right side of the Facebook toolbar.

2 Select **Privacy Settings** to display the Privacy Settings page.

3 Scroll to the Control Your Default Privacy section and select from one of the three available options: **Public**, **Friends**, or **Custom**.

Continued

## NOTE

**Public Sharing** Facebook makes your information and status updates public by default. This is because Facebook believes it can better connect users with one another and build a stronger community by making public all of a user's likes and dislikes. The more Facebook knows about you, the more connections it can recommend and make. ■

## TIP

**Custom Sharing** The Custom option is probably more useful when applied on a post-by-post basis. Use the Custom option when you post a status update you only want to share with close friends, or don't want to an uploaded photograph with co-workers, or the like. ■

4 If you select Custom, you see the Custom Privacy dialog box. To hide your information from everyone, pull down the **Make This Visible To** list and select **Only Me**.

5 To make your information visible only to specific people, pull down the **Make This Visible To** list, select **Specific People or Lists**, and then enter the names of those Facebook users (or the name of a custom friends list) you want to see the info.

6 To hide your information only from specific people, enter their names into the **Hide This From These People or Lists** box.

7 Click the **Save Changes** button when done.

*End*

**TIP**

**Post-by-Post Privacy** Remember, you can also determine who can view your status updates on a post-by-post basis. When you enter a new status update, click the **Privacy** button (down arrow) beneath the text box; click this to display the privacy menu of **Public**, **Friends**, or **Custom**. Make your selection, and this particular post is only viewable by the group you select. ■

**NOTE**

**Company and School Networks** If you're a member of a company or school network, you'll also have the option of making an item visible to or hiding it from members of that network. ■

# CONTROLLING HOW YOU CONNECT

How much of your personal information can people see on Facebook? And just who can contact you on the Facebook site—and how? It's all a matter of how you configure Facebook's connect settings.

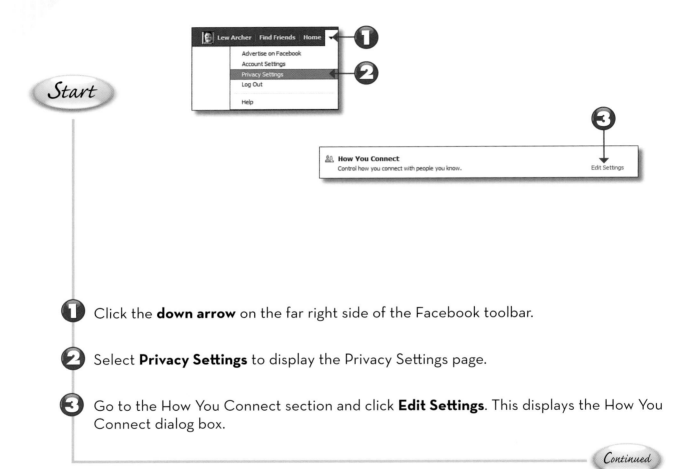

**Start**

① Click the **down arrow** on the far right side of the Facebook toolbar.

② Select **Privacy Settings** to display the Privacy Settings page.

③ Go to the How You Connect section and click **Edit Settings**. This displays the How You Connect dialog box.

Continued

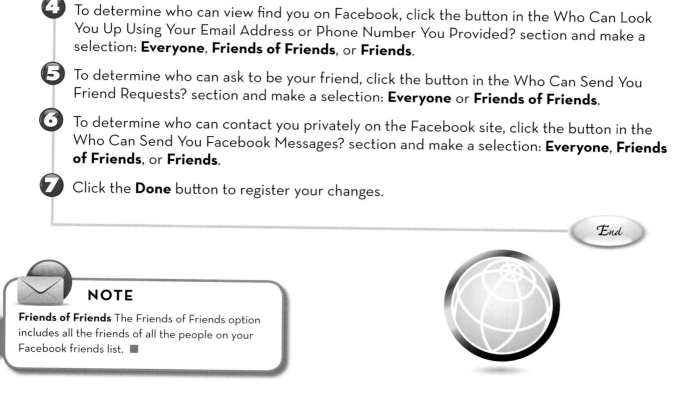

**4** To determine who can view find you on Facebook, click the button in the Who Can Look You Up Using Your Email Address or Phone Number You Provided? section and make a selection: **Everyone**, **Friends of Friends**, or **Friends**.

**5** To determine who can ask to be your friend, click the button in the Who Can Send You Friend Requests? section and make a selection: **Everyone** or **Friends of Friends**.

**6** To determine who can contact you privately on the Facebook site, click the button in the Who Can Send You Facebook Messages? section and make a selection: **Everyone**, **Friends of Friends**, or **Friends**.

**7** Click the **Done** button to register your changes.

*End*

**NOTE**

**Friends of Friends** The Friends of Friends option includes all the friends of all the people on your Facebook friends list. ■

# CONTROLLING TIMELINE POSTS AND TAGS

Next up are those settings that affect who can post and who can see those posts on your timeline page. Also important is what happens when someone tags you in one of their photos.

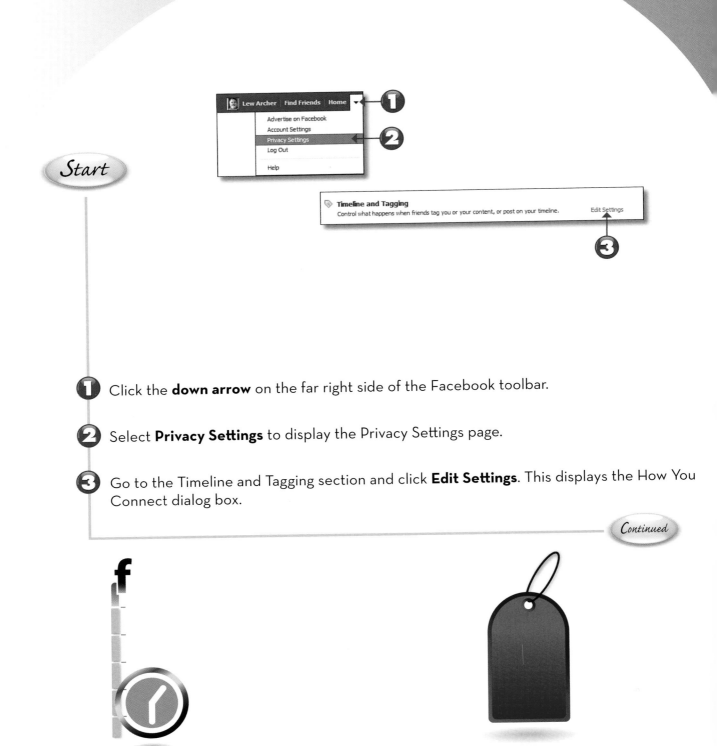

Start

**1** Click the **down arrow** on the far right side of the Facebook toolbar.

**2** Select **Privacy Settings** to display the Privacy Settings page.

**3** Go to the Timeline and Tagging section and click **Edit Settings**. This displays the How You Connect dialog box.

Continued

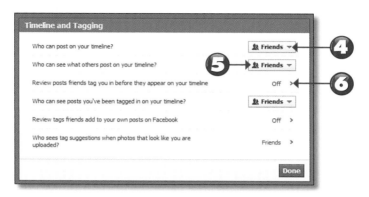

**4** To control who can post on your timeline, click the button in the Who Can Post in Your Timeline? section and make a selection: **Friends** or **No One**.

**5** To control who can see the posts that others make on your timeline, click the button in the Who Can See What Others Post on Your Timeline? section and make a selection: **Everyone**, **Friends of Friends**, **Friends**, or **Custom**.

**6** If you want to personally approve or reject all posts in which friends have tagged you, go to the Review Posts Friends Tag You In Before They Appear on Your Timeline section and click the **Off** option to turn it on.

*Continued*

**CAUTION**

**Timeline Review** Even if you enable the review of tagged posts and reject a tag, the post is still made; it just doesn't appear on your timeline page. The picture or post can still be viewed on your friends' timeline, which still exposes you publicly.

**Timeline and Tagging**

Who can post on your timeline?                                                          &#x1F465; Friends ▾

Who can see what others post on your timeline?                                          &#x1F465; Friends ▾

Review posts friends tag you in before they appear on your timeline                    Off   ›

Who can see posts you've been tagged in on your timeline?                              &#x1F465; Friends ▾          **7**

Review tags friends add to your own posts on Facebook                   **8**→ Off   ›

Who sees tag suggestions when photos that look like you are
uploaded?                                                                               Friends  ›

Done

**7** To determine who can see posts on your timeline from others who have tagged you, go to the Who Can See Posts You've Been Tagged in on Your Timeline? section and make a selection: **Everyone**, **Friends of Friends**, **Friends**, or **Custom**.

**8** To personally review all tags your friends add to your posts, go to the Review Tags Friends Add to Your Own Posts on Facebook section and click the **Off** option to turn it on.

*Continued*

**NOTE**

**Tag Review** When someone creates a tag that you then need to review, you receive a notification via email and on the Notifications menu on the Facebook toolbar. ■

**Timeline and Tagging**

Who can post on your timeline? · 👥 Friends ▾

Who can see what others post on your timeline? · 👥 Friends ▾

Review posts friends tag you in before they appear on your timeline · Off ›

Who can see posts you've been tagged in on your timeline? · 👥 Friends ▾

Review tags friends add to your own posts on Facebook · Off ›

Who sees tag suggestions when photos that look like you are uploaded? · Friends ✕ ⟵ **9**

Done ⟵ **12**

**Tag Suggestions**

When a photo that looks like you is uploaded, we'll suggest adding a tag of you. This helps save time when adding tags to photos, especially when labeling many photos from one event. Suggestions can always be ignored and no one will be tagged automatically.

Who sees tag suggestions when photos that look like you are uploaded? · Friends ▾ ⟵ **10**

Learn more · Okay ⟵ **11**

**9** To determine who can see the tag suggestions when they upload photos of you, click the option in the Who Sees Tag Suggestions When Photos That Look Like You Are Uploaded? section to display the Tag Suggestions dialog box.

**10** Click the **Privacy** button and select either **Friends** or **No One**.

**11** Click the **Okay** button to close the Tag Suggestion dialog box.

**12** Click the **Done** button to close the Timeline and Tagging dialog box.

*End*

### NOTE

**Face Recognition** The tag suggestions made by Facebook when someone uploads a picture of someone who looks like you are enabled by special face-recognition technology. ■

# CONTROLLING WHAT GETS SHARED WITH ADS, APPS, AND OTHER WEBSITES

Facebook shares a lot of information with its advertisers, to better personalize the ads it serves to users. It also shares information with third-party apps and with other websites—particularly those you log in to with your Facebook ID. Fortunately, you can stop any or all of this information sharing, if you like.

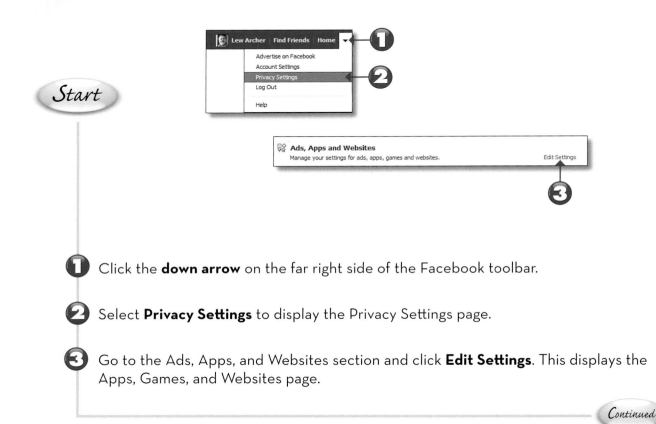

*Start*

**1** Click the **down arrow** on the far right side of the Facebook toolbar.

**2** Select **Privacy Settings** to display the Privacy Settings page.

**3** Go to the Ads, Apps, and Websites section and click **Edit Settings**. This displays the Apps, Games, and Websites page.

*Continued*

**NOTE**

**Open Graph** Facebook likes to shares your personal data with partner websites, in the guise of helping those sites "personalize" their content for you. This sharing is part of Facebook's Open Graph protocol, which helps other sites link to the Facebook site. This can come in the form of a common sign-in (you log in to the other site using your Facebook ID and password), a Facebook Like button on the other site, or the wholesale sharing of information about you between the two sites. ■

**CAUTION**

**Caution** Limiting information sharing with third parties may impact your ability to use those third-party apps or to take advantage of all the sharing options from some websites. ■

**4** To edit the settings for the individual apps you use on Facebook, go to the Apps You Use section and click the **Edit Settings** button. You now see a list of all the Facebook apps you've used.

**5** To delete a given app, click the **X** to the far right of the app's name.

**6** To edit the privacy and notifications for a given app, click the **Edit** link to the right of that app's name. This expands the edit panel for that app.

**7** Edit the app's settings as necessary and then click the **Close** button.

*Continued*

**NOTE**

**App Settings** The settings for each app are unique. You may find settings to determine who can see an app's posts, how the app can notify you, and what information that app can access. ■

How people bring your info to apps they use | People who can see your info can bring it with them when they use apps. Use this setting to control the categories of information people can bring with them. | **Edit Settings**

**How people bring your info to apps they use**

People on Facebook who can see your info can bring it with them when they use apps. This makes their experience better and more social. Use the settings below to control the categories of information that people can bring with them when they use apps, games and websites.

☑ Bio
☑ Birthday
☑ Family and relationships
☐ Interested in
☐ Religious and political views
☑ My website
☑ If I'm online
☑ My status updates
☑ My photos

☑ My videos
☑ My links
☑ My notes
☑ Hometown
☑ Current city
☑ Education and work
☑ Activities, interests, things I like
☑ My app activity

If you don't want apps and websites to access other categories of information (like your friend list, gender or info you've made public), you can turn off all Platform apps. But remember, you will not be able to use any games or apps yourself.

**Save Changes** | **Cancel**

(8) To determine which of your personal information your friends can share with the apps they use, go to the How People Bring Your Info into Apps They Use section and click the **Edit Settings** button to display the corresponding dialog box.

(9) Check those items you want your friends to share and uncheck those you don't.

(10) Click the **Save Changes** button when done.

*Continued*

**NOTE**

**Sharing Info** Facebook would like your friends' apps to have access to all your personal information, including your bio, birthday, family relationships, interests, status updates, photos, and the like. In reality, the more personal info you allow shared, the more easily your friends' apps can target you for promotion and advertising. ■

**TIP**

**The More You Share** The more info you let your friends share, the more social your experience on Facebook. The less info you share, the more protected your privacy. ■

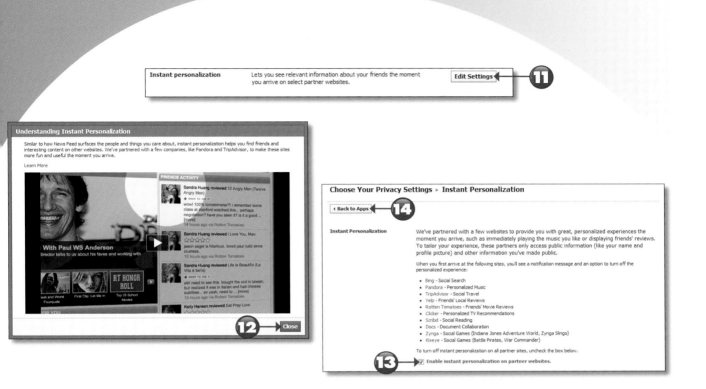

 **To disable the sharing of your personal information with third-party websites, such as Pandora and TripAdvisor, go to the Instant Personalization section and click the **Edit Settings** button.**

**Facebook now displays video explaining why instant personalization is such a great deal for you. Play it if you like or click the **Close** button to proceed with what you really want to do.**

**When the Instant Personalization page finally appears, uncheck the **Enable Instant Personalization on Partner Websites** option.**

**Click the **Back to Apps** button to return to the Apps, Games, and Websites page.**

Continued

### TIP

**Don't Use Your Facebook ID** Here's a simpler way to make sure Facebook doesn't share your private information with other websites: Don't log in to these sites with your Facebook account! When you go to a site and you're prompted to use your Facebook ID to log in, don't do it. Instead, create a separate ID for that site, unrelated to your Facebook log in. ■

### TIP

**No Thanks** If, when you visit a website, you see a blue bar at the top of the page informing you that this site is using Facebook "to personalize your experience," you also see a No Thanks link in the bar. Click **No Thanks**, and the site doesn't use your Facebook data. ■

| Public search | Show a preview of your Facebook timeline when people look for you using a search engine. | Edit Settings | 15 |
| Ads | Manage settings for third-party and social ads. | Edit Settings | 18 |

**Choose Your Privacy Settings ▸ Public Search**

‹ Back to Apps  17

Public search — Public search controls whether people who enter your name in a search engine will see a preview of your Facebook timeline. Because some search engines cache information, some of your timeline information may be available for a period of time after you turn public search off. See preview

16 → ☑ Enable public search

**15** If you don't want your Facebook timeline and information to be visible to Google and other search engines, go to the Public Search section and click the **Edit Settings** button.

**16** When the Public Search page appears, uncheck the **Enable Public Search** option.

**17** Click the **Back to Apps** button to return to the Apps, Games, and Websites page.

**18** To limit the amount of personal information Facebook shares with advertisers on its site, go to the Ads section and click **Edit Settings**.

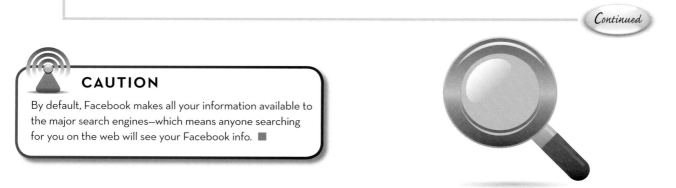

*Continued*

## CAUTION

By default, Facebook makes all your information available to the major search engines—which means anyone searching for you on the web will see your Facebook info. ■

**Facebook Ads**

**A Note About Your Photos**
There's a false rumor circulating that Facebook is changing who owns your content and how it's used. You own all of the content and information you post on Facebook. Please see our Statement of Rights and Responsibilities for more information.

**Ads shown by third parties**
Facebook does not give third party applications or ad networks the right to use your name or picture in ads. If we allow this in the future, the setting you choose will determine how your information is used.

You may see social context on third party sites, including in ads, through Facebook social plugins. Although social plugins enable you to have a social experience on a third party site, Facebook does not share your information with the third party sites hosting the social plugins. Learn more about social plugins.

Edit third party ad settings ← **19**

**Ads and friends**
Everyone wants to know what their friends like. That's why we pair ads and friends—an easy wa
what your friends share and like. Learn more about social ads.

Here are the facts:
- Social ads show an advertiser's message alongside actions you have taken, such as liking a P
- Your privacy settings apply to social ads
- We don't sell your information to advertisers
- Only confirmed friends can see your actions alongside an ad
- If a photo is used, it is your pro... hoto and not from your photo albums

Edit social ads setting ← **21**

---

**Ads and friends**
Everyone wants to know what their friends like. That's why we pair ads and friends—an easy way to find products and services you're interested in, based on what your friends share and like. Learn more about social ads.

Here are the facts:
- Social ads show an advertiser's message alongside actions you have taken, such as liking a Page
- Your privacy settings apply to social ads
- We don't sell your information to advertisers
- Only confirmed friends can see your actions alongside an ad
- If a photo is used, it is your profile photo and not from your photo albums

**Here's an example of a Facebook Ad:**

**Denver Sushi**
The best sushi in Denver. Try our daily lunch specials for $9.95. Fan our page for special offers.

**Denver Sushi**
The best sushi in Denver. Try our daily lunch specials for $9.95. Fan our page for special offers.

👍 Like · Lew Archer likes this.

This setting only applies to ads that we pair with news about social actions. So, independent of this setting, you may still see social actions in other contexts, like in Sponsored Stories or paired with messages from Facebook. You can learn more about how social ads, Sponsored Stories, and messages from Facebook work in the Help Center.

Pair my social actions with ads for  No one ▾

**Save Changes**  Cancel

---

**Ads shown by third parties**
Facebook does not give third party applications or ad networks the right to use your name or picture in ads. If we allow this in choose will determine how your information is used.

You may see social context on third party sites, including in ads, through Facebook social plugins. Although social plugins enab experience on a third party site, Facebook does not share your information with the third party sites hosting the social plugins plugins.

If we allow this in the future, show my information to  No one ▾

**Save Changes**  Cancel

**20**

**22**

---

**19** To block information sharing with third-party advertisers, click **Edit Third Party Ad Settings**.

**20** Pull down the list and select to show your information to **No One** and then click the **Save Changes** button.

**21** To block information sharing on so-called social ads, click **Edit Social Ads Sharing**.

**22** Pull down the list and select pair your social actions with ads for **No One** and then click the **Save Changes** button.

*End*

**NOTE**

**Third-Party Ads** Facebook does not at present allow third-party advertisers to use your name or picture in their ads. The third-party ad settings affect what Facebook may or may not do in the future. ■

**NOTE**

**Social Ads** A social ad incorporates your personal information and actions into ads displayed to your friends. For example, if you've liked an advertiser's Facebook page, your picture may show up in an ad that says you recommend that advertiser's products. ■

# LIMITING WHO CAN SEE OLD POSTS

By default, old information you've shared publicly on Facebook stays public. If you'd rather limit the availability of this information going forward, you can limit the audience for these old posts to just your friends.

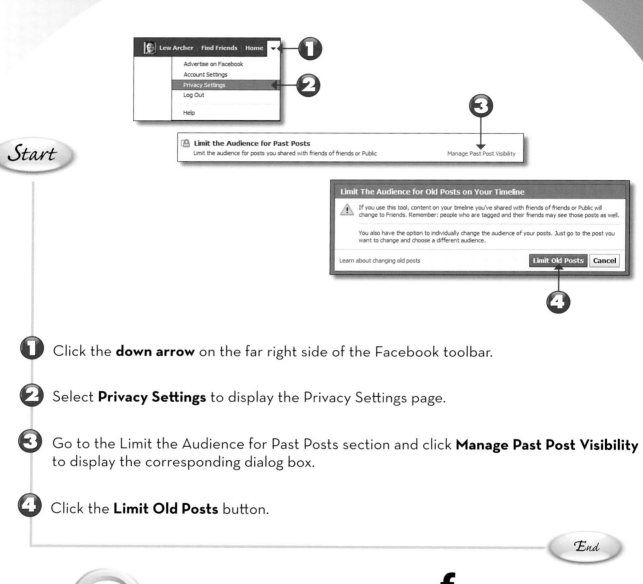

**1** Click the **down arrow** on the far right side of the Facebook toolbar.

**2** Select **Privacy Settings** to display the Privacy Settings page.

**3** Go to the Limit the Audience for Past Posts section and click **Manage Past Post Visibility** to display the corresponding dialog box.

**4** Click the **Limit Old Posts** button.

Chapter 14

# MANAGING YOUR FACEBOOK ACCOUNT

Your Facebook account contains your basic personal information—your name, email address, password, and the like. What do you do if you change your name upon getting married, or after a divorce (or remarriage), or upon getting a new email account or finding that your password is compromised? Fortunately, Facebook lets you easily change any and all of this information, at any time.

# EDITING ACCOUNT SETTINGS

Click to display general settings

| | General Account Settings | |
|---|---|---|
| ⚙ **General** | | |
| 🛡 Security | | |
| 🗨 Notifications | **Name** | Lew Archer | Edit |
| 📇 Subscribers | **Username** | http://www.facebook.com/**LewArcherDetective** | Edit |
| 🎮 Apps | **Email** | Primary: **lewarcher2010@gmail.com** | Edit |
| 📱 Mobile | **Password** | Password never changed. | Edit |
| 💳 Payments | **Networks** | No networks. | Edit |
| 🎫 Facebook Ads | **Language** | English (US) | Edit |
| You can also visit your privacy settings or edit your timeline to control who sees the info there. | Download a copy of your Facebook data. | |

Click to edit specific settings

# CHANGING YOUR ACCOUNT SETTINGS

You can change all your Facebook settings from the Account Settings page, which you access from the Facebook toolbar. The Account Settings page has eight different tabs, each of which hosts a specific type of information.

**Start**

① Click the **down arrow** on the far right of the Facebook toolbar.

② Click **Account Settings** from the pull-down menu to display the Account Settings page.

③ To change general accounts settings (username, email address, password, and so on), click the **General** tab.

④ Click **Edit** for each item you want to edit. Make your changes and then click the **Save Changes** button.

Continued

---

**NOTE**

**General Settings** The settings on the General tab include Name, Username, Email, Password, Networks (for school and work), and Language. ■

**TIP**

**Changing Passwords** It's a good idea to change your Facebook password every month or two. This decreases the possibility of your account password being hacked. ■

**Security Settings**

| | | |
|---|---|---|
| **Security Question** | Setting a security question will help us identify you. | Edit |
| **Secure Browsing** | Secure browsing is currently **disabled.** | Edit |
| **Login Notifications** | Login notifications are **disabled.** | Edit |
| **Login Approvals** | Approval is **not required** when logging in from an unrecognized device. | Edit |
| **App Passwords** | You haven't created App Passwords. | Edit |
| **Recognized Devices** | No recognized devices. | Edit |
| **Active Sessions** | Logged in from **St Charles, IL, US** and 9 other locations. | Edit |

Deactivate your account.

**Notifications Settings**

We send notifications whenever actions are taken on Facebook that involve you. You can change which applications and features can send you notifications. Notifications are being sent to **lewarcher2010@gmail.com** (email).

**Recent Notifications**

**All Notifications**

| | | |
|---|---|---|
| Facebook | 18 | Edit |
| Photos | 8 | Edit |
| Groups | 6 | Edit |
| Pages | 3 | Edit |
| Events | 9 | Edit |
| Questions | 5 | Edit |

**5** To change settings related to your system security, click the **Security** tab.

**6** To change how and when Facebook sends you notifications about various events, click the **Notifications** tab.

*Continued*

**NOTE**

**Security Settings** The settings on the Security tab include Secure Browsing, Login Notifications, Login Approvals, App Passwords, Recognized Devices, and Active Sessions. You can also deactivate your Facebook account from this page. ■

**TIP**

**Recent Notifications** The Notifications tab also displays your most recent notifications sent today and this week. ■

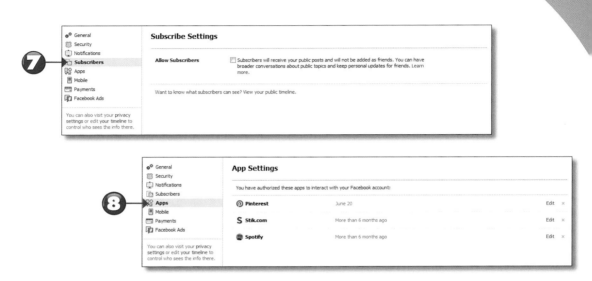

 To let people subscribe to your posts without becoming friends and to manage subscription options, click the **Subscribers** tab.

 To edit the settings for the various Facebook apps you use and to delete selected apps, click the **Apps** tab.

*Continued*

**NOTE**

**Subscriber Settings** The settings on the Subscribers tab include Allow Subscribers, Subscriber Comments, Subscriber Notifications, Username, and Twitter (to connect a Twitter account). ◾

**TIP**

**Facebook Subscribers** Facebook's subscriber feature is more suited to companies or public individuals with Facebook pages. Fans and followers can subscribe to these pages without having to be "friended" by the company or individual. ◾

**9** To set up your account for use with your mobile phone, click the **Mobile** tab.

**10** Some Facebook apps and games use Facebook Credits as currency. To manage your Facebook currency and payments, click the **Payments** tab.

**11** To manage how third-party advertisers can use your personal information in their ads, click the **Facebook Ads** tab.

*End*

### NOTE

**Linking Mobile Phones** To link your mobile phone to your Facebook account, Facebook will send a confirmation code via text message to your phone. After you enter that code into the Confirmation Code box on the Mobile tab, this phone will be linked to your specific Facebook account. ■

### TIP

**Mobile Facebook** After you've linked your mobile phone to your Facebook account, you can configure Facebook to send selected notifications to your phone as text messages. You can also post new status updates from your phone via text messaging. ■

# DEACTIVATING YOUR FACEBOOK ACCOUNT

If you ever choose to leave Facebook, you have two options. You can *deactivate* your account, which temporarily hides your account information from others; or you can *delete* your account, which permanently removes your account information.

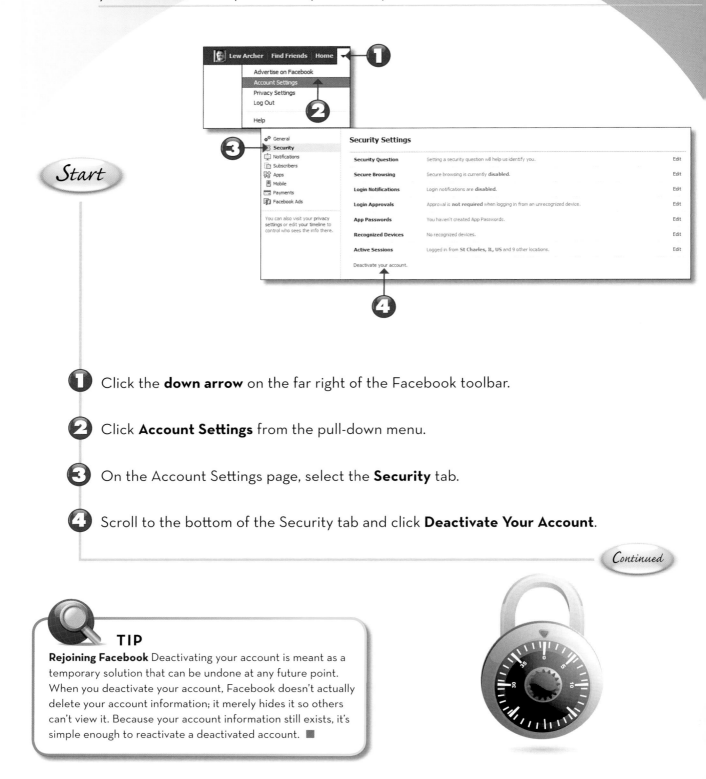

1. Click the **down arrow** on the far right of the Facebook toolbar.

2. Click **Account Settings** from the pull-down menu.

3. On the Account Settings page, select the **Security** tab.

4. Scroll to the bottom of the Security tab and click **Deactivate Your Account**.

Continued

## TIP

**Rejoining Facebook** Deactivating your account is meant as a temporary solution that can be undone at any future point. When you deactivate your account, Facebook doesn't actually delete your account information; it merely hides it so others can't view it. Because your account information still exists, it's simple enough to reactivate a deactivated account. ■

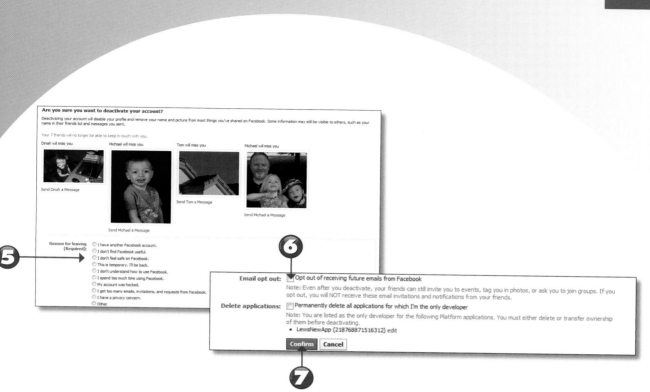

**5** On the next page, scroll to the Reason for Leaving section and select just why it is you're leaving. This is a requirement; you have to tell Facebook something here.

**6** If you don't want to be hounded by Facebook to venture back into the fold, check the **Opt Out of Receiving Future Emails from Facebook** box.

**7** Click the **Confirm** button to deactivate your account.

*End*

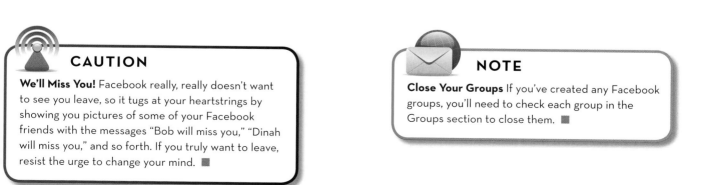

### CAUTION

**We'll Miss You!** Facebook really, really doesn't want to see you leave, so it tugs at your heartstrings by showing you pictures of some of your Facebook friends with the messages "Bob will miss you," "Dinah will miss you," and so forth. If you truly want to leave, resist the urge to change your mind. ■

### NOTE

**Close Your Groups** If you've created any Facebook groups, you'll need to check each group in the Groups section to close them. ■

# DELETING YOUR FACEBOOK ACCOUNT

If you're absolutely, positively sure you'll never want to be a Facebook user again—and you want more reassurance that your personal data has been wiped—then you want to permanently delete your account. This is more difficult to do than deactivating your account, for the simple reason that your Facebook account is likely connected to lots of other websites.

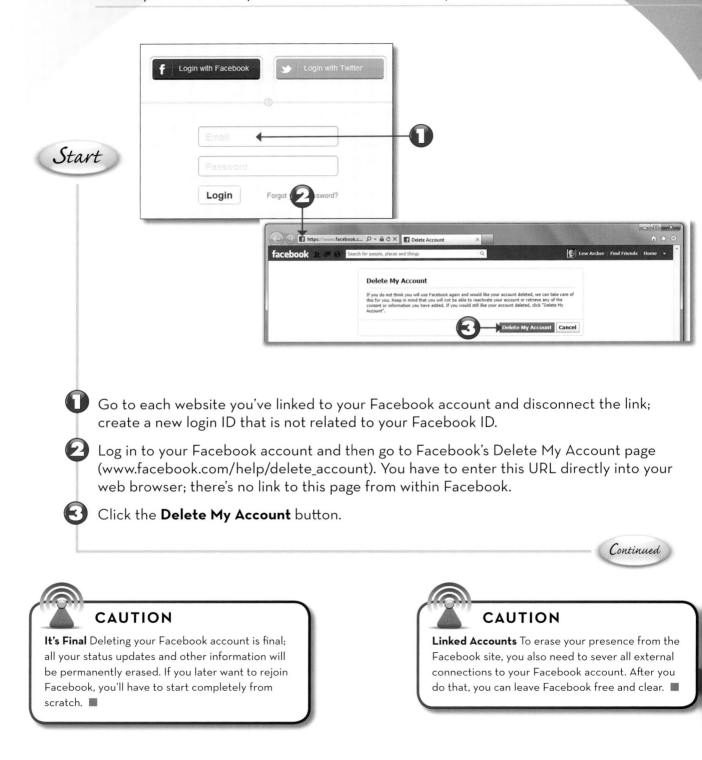

**1** Go to each website you've linked to your Facebook account and disconnect the link; create a new login ID that is not related to your Facebook ID.

**2** Log in to your Facebook account and then go to Facebook's Delete My Account page (www.facebook.com/help/delete_account). You have to enter this URL directly into your web browser; there's no link to this page from within Facebook.

**3** Click the **Delete My Account** button.

Continued

**CAUTION**

**It's Final** Deleting your Facebook account is final; all your status updates and other information will be permanently erased. If you later want to rejoin Facebook, you'll have to start completely from scratch. ■

**CAUTION**

**Linked Accounts** To erase your presence from the Facebook site, you also need to sever all external connections to your Facebook account. After you do that, you can leave Facebook free and clear. ■

 This displays the Permanently Delete Account dialog box. Enter your Facebook password into the Password box.

Enter the displayed characters into the Security Check box.

Click the **Okay** button.

End

## CAUTION

**14 Days** When you follow this procedure, Facebook will delete your account—so long as you don't log back in to Facebook for the next 14 days. Any interaction with your Facebook account during this 14-day period reactivates your account. This also means not logging in to any other websites connected to your Facebook account or clicking the Facebook Like button on any other website. ■

*Chapter 15*

# USING FACEBOOK ON THE GO

Many people connect with Facebook from their personal computers, but that isn't the only way to do it. You can also use your mobile phone to post status updates and read posts in your Facebook news feed. Connecting in this fashion helps you keep in touch while you're on the go—or just waiting in line at the supermarket.

You can connect to Facebook from any mobile phone, using simple text messages. But if you have a smartphone, like the Apple iPhone, you can use phone-specific Facebook applications to gain access to most of Facebook's features on the go. In this chapter, we examine how to use Facebook via Facebook's iPhone app—one of the most popular apps for the most popular smartphone today.

# IPHONE APP'S HOME SCREEN

Search Facebook —

Display your
timeline page

Display the
news feed

Read messages —

See friends nearby —

View upcoming events —

Browse for
Facebook apps

# NAVIGATING FACEBOOK'S IPHONE APP

Facebook's iPhone app is a full-featured interface for Facebook on your smartphone. You can find the Facebook app in apple's iPhone App Store; just search the store for "Facebook" and then download the app—it's free.

*Start*

1 When you launch Facebook's iPhone app, you're taken immediately to the News Feed screen. Tap the **Friend Requests** icon on the toolbar to view all pending friend requests.

2 Tap the **Messages** button on the toolbar to view new messages.

3 Tap the **Notifications** button on the toolbar to view new notifications.

4 Access other site features by tapping the **Menu** button at the far left of the toolbar.

*Continued*

**NOTE**

**Logging In** The first time you launch the Facebook app, you need to enter your email address and password to log in to the Facebook site. ▪

**TIP**

**Pending Notifications** If you have any pending friend requests, messages, or notifications, you'll see a red number on top of that item's icon on the toolbar. The number signifies how many messages, notifications, and so on that you have pending. ▪

**5** Search Facebook by entering a query into the Search box.

**6** Tap one of the Favorites items to view that information.

**7** Tap the **Menu** button to return to the News Feed screen.

*End*

**NOTE**

**Learn More** Learn more about Facebook for iPhone by going to the app's Facebook page at www.facebook.com/appcenter/fbiphone. ■

**NOTE**

**Other Smartphones** The iPhone isn't the only smartphone or tablet supported by Facebook. There are Facebook apps for Android, Blackberry, INQ, Nokia, Palm, Sidekick, Sony Ericsson, and Windows Mobile devices. You can also connect your web-enabled phone directly to Facebook's mobile website, at m.facebook.com. ■

# VIEWING THE NEWS FEED

To display the news feed, tap the **News Feed** icon on the Home screen. Like the computer version of the news feed, this screen is divided into Top Stories and Recent Stories; scroll down the screen to view more posts. Each post in the mobile news feed is similar to what you see on the web-based news feed—you see the name of the poster, the post itself, and any photos or other attachments.

Start

 To view a poster's timeline page, tap that person's name.

 If there are links within the post, tapping a link opens the linked-to web page in a new screen.

 If a post has a picture attached, tap the picture to view it fullscreen.

*Continued*

**TIP**

**Refreshing** To refresh the news feed, scroll to the very top of the page, and then pull the page down. You should see an Updating pane before the news feed is refreshed. ■

**TIP**

**Sorting** By default, the news feed is sorted with top stories first. If you'd rather see the most recent posts first, tap the **Sort** button and select **Most Recent**. ■

**4** To "like" a post, tap **Like**.

**5** To comment on a post, tap **Comment** to display the Comment screen.

**6** Use the onscreen keyboard to type your comment.

**7** Tap the **Post** button.

*End*

**TIP**

**Likes** The number of likes a post has received is indicated by the number next to the thumbs-up icon. ■

**TIP**

**Comments** To read other comments, tap the **Comments** (word balloon) icon. ■

# POSTING A STATUS UPDATE

The iPhone's Facebook app lets you easily post status updates from wherever you happen to be at the time. It's a great way to let your friends know what you're doing, and where.

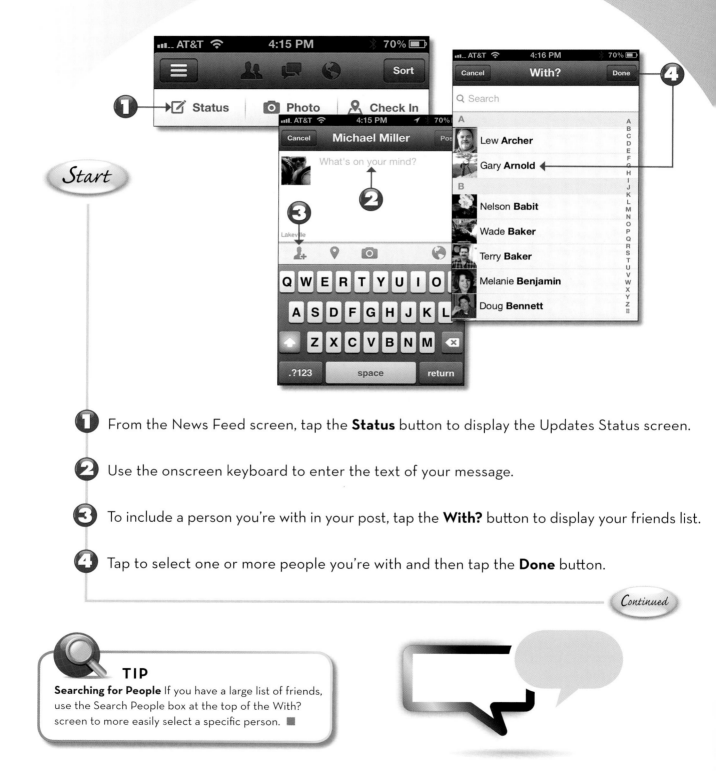

**1** From the News Feed screen, tap the **Status** button to display the Updates Status screen.

**2** Use the onscreen keyboard to enter the text of your message.

**3** To include a person you're with in your post, tap the **With?** button to display your friends list.

**4** Tap to select one or more people you're with and then tap the **Done** button.

*Continued*

### TIP

**Searching for People** If you have a large list of friends, use the Search People box at the top of the With? screen to more easily select a specific person. ■

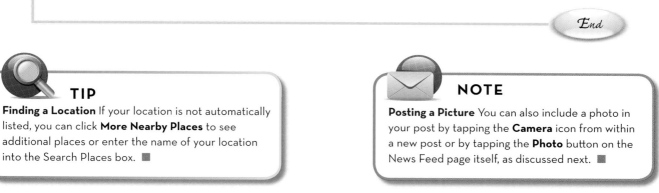

**5** To tag this update from a specific location, tap the **Where Are You?** button to display a list of nearby locations.

**6** Tap your current location.

**7** To determine who can view this post, tap the **Privacy** button and select from one of the available options: **Public**, **Friends**, or **Only Me**.

**8** Tap the **Post** button to post your status update.

*End*

**TIP**

**Finding a Location** If your location is not automatically listed, you can click **More Nearby Places** to see additional places or enter the name of your location into the Search Places box. ■

**NOTE**

**Posting a Picture** You can also include a photo in your post by tapping the **Camera** icon from within a new post or by tapping the **Photo** button on the News Feed page itself, as discussed next. ■

# TAKING AND POSTING A PICTURE

Facebook's iPhone app lets you post pictures directly from your smartphone. You can post pictures already stored in your Photos library or take a new picture with your iPhone's built-in camera.

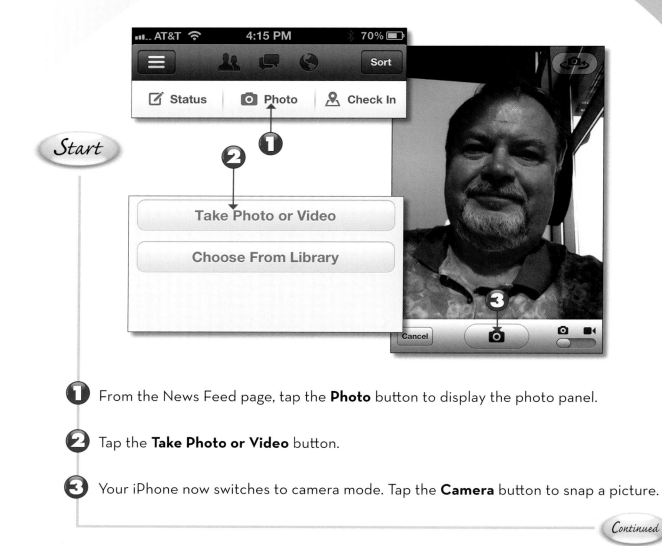

**Start**

① From the News Feed page, tap the **Photo** button to display the photo panel.

② Tap the **Take Photo or Video** button.

③ Your iPhone now switches to camera mode. Tap the **Camera** button to snap a picture.

Continued

**TIP**

**Self-Portraits** To take a picture of yourself, tap the button at the top right of the camera screen. This switches the iPhone to the self-facing camera, aimed right at your smiling face. ■

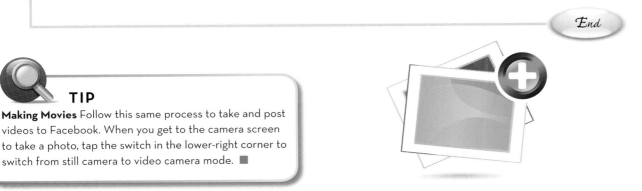

**4** You now see the Preview screen. If you like what you see, tap the **Use** button.

**5** When the next screen appears, if there's a face in the picture, tap a face to tag that person, and then tap the **Use** button.

**6** You now see the Add Photos screen with a new status updated started. Complete the status update by adding a text message, people you're with, where you're with, and privacy settings.

**7** Tap the **Post** button to post the photo.

*End*

### TIP
**Making Movies** Follow this same process to take and post videos to Facebook. When you get to the camera screen to take a photo, tap the switch in the lower-right corner to switch from still camera to video camera mode. ■

# POSTING A PICTURE FROM YOUR LIBRARY

You can also post photos that you've already taken and stored in your iPhone's Photos library. The process is similar to posting a newly taken photo.

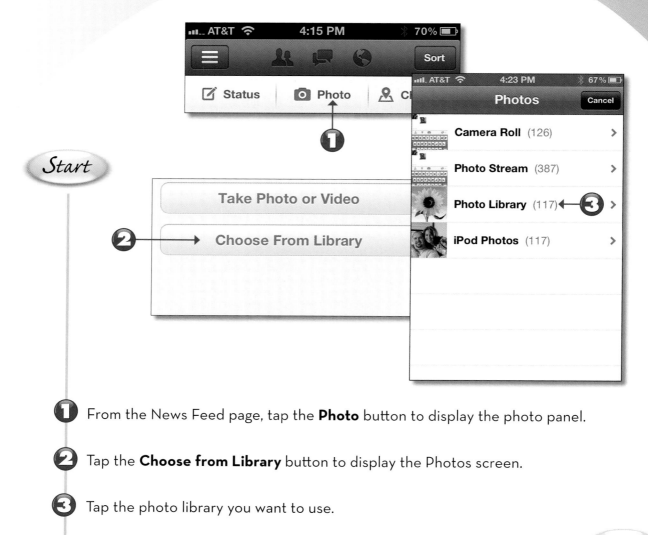

1. From the News Feed page, tap the **Photo** button to display the photo panel.

2. Tap the **Choose from Library** button to display the Photos screen.

3. Tap the photo library you want to use.

Continued

**NOTE**

**One per Post** The iPhone app only lets you include one picture per status update. ■

**4** Tap the picture you want to post.

**5** When the next screen appears, tap a face to tag a person in your photo and then tap the **Use** button.

**6** You now see the Add Photos screen with a new status updated started. Complete the status update by adding a text message, people you're with, where you're with, and privacy settings.

**7** Tap the **Post** button to post the photo.

*End*

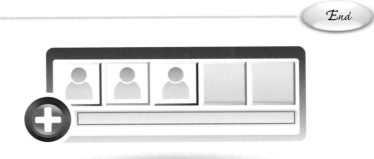

# CHECKING IN WITH YOUR CURRENT LOCATION

Because you're likely using Facebook's iPhone app while you're out and about, you can use the app to let your friends know where you are. This is done via the Check In feature, which posts a quick and easy update with your current location entered.

*Start*

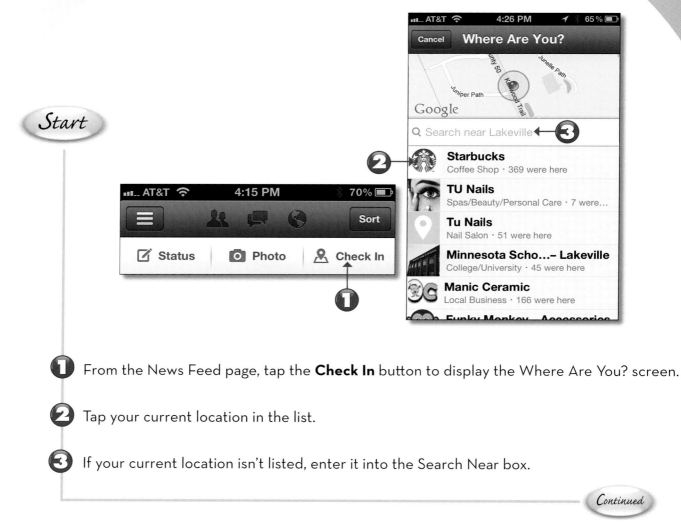

1. From the News Feed page, tap the **Check In** button to display the Where Are You? screen.

2. Tap your current location in the list.

3. If your current location isn't listed, enter it into the Search Near box.

*Continued*

*Continued*

## CAUTION

**Beware Stalkers** Using the Check In feature to broadcast your current location can alert any potential stalkers where to find you—or tell potential burglars that your house is currently empty. Because of the potential dangers, think twice about using this feature. ■

**4** You now see the Post screen with a new status updated started. Complete the status update by adding a text message if you like, as well as people you're with and privacy settings.

**5** Tap the **Post** button to post your location.

*End*

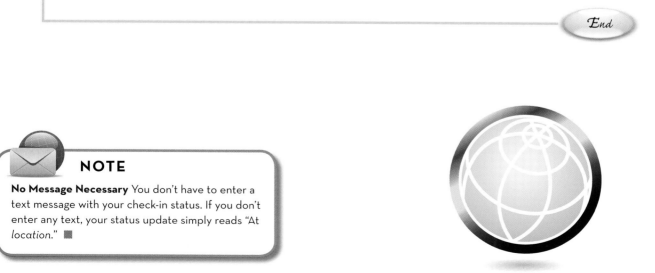

### NOTE

**No Message Necessary** You don't have to enter a text message with your check-in status. If you don't enter any text, your status update simply reads "At *location*." ■

# VIEWING A FRIEND'S TIMELINE

You can view any person's timeline page on your iPhone, just as you would on your computer. Note, however, that the iPhone timeline is a little different than the one you see on your (larger) computer screen.

*Start*

**1** Tap your friend's name anywhere on the Facebook site to display his or her timeline page.

**2** Your friend's basic information is displayed at the top of the page. To display more personal information, tap **About**.

*Continued*

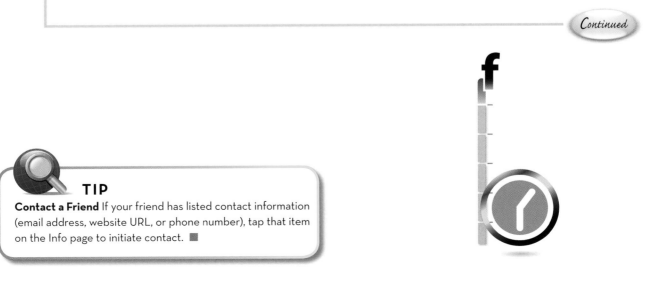

## TIP

**Contact a Friend** If your friend has listed contact information (email address, website URL, or phone number), tap that item on the Info page to initiate contact. ■

**3** To view your friend's status updates and life events, scroll down the screen.

**4** To post a message on your friend's timeline page, tap the **Write Post** button.

**5** To view your friend's photos, tap the **Photos** button.

**6** Tap the **Albums** button to view your friend's photo albums and then tap an album to view all the pictures within.

*End*

**TIP**

**Share a Photo** To share a photo with your friend, go to his Timeline and tap the **Share Photo** button. ■

# CHECKING YOUR MESSAGES

You can use your iPhone to check your Facebook messages while you're on the go. If you have private messages from other users, they'll show up in your Facebook inbox.

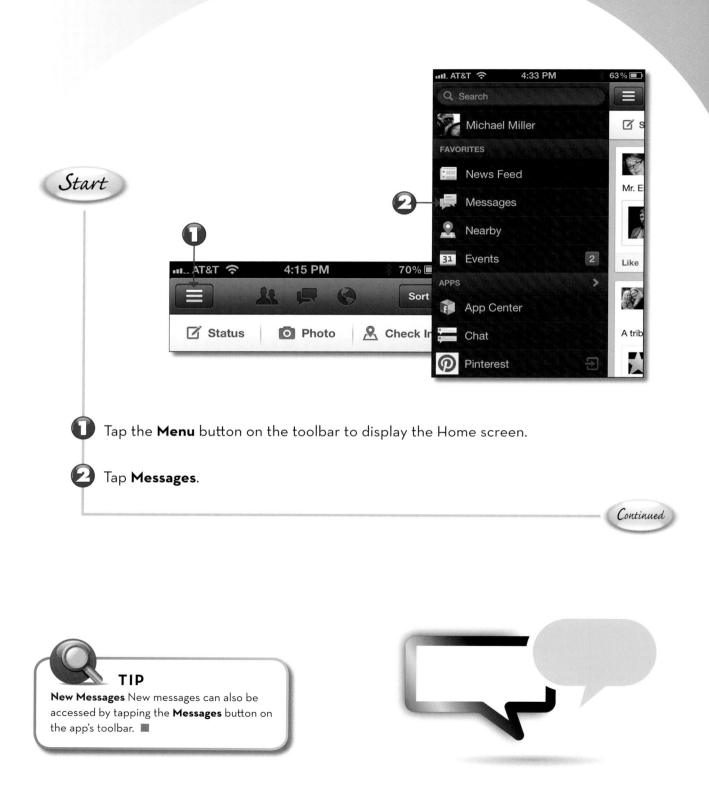

1. Tap the **Menu** button on the toolbar to display the Home screen.

2. Tap **Messages**.

Continued

**TIP**

**New Messages** New messages can also be accessed by tapping the **Messages** button on the app's toolbar. ■

**3** You now see a list of messages, grouped by sender. To view all messages (including chats) from a given user, tap that person's name.

**4** To reply to the latest message from this person, enter your text into the Write a Reply box.

**5** Tap the **Send** button to send your reply.

*End*

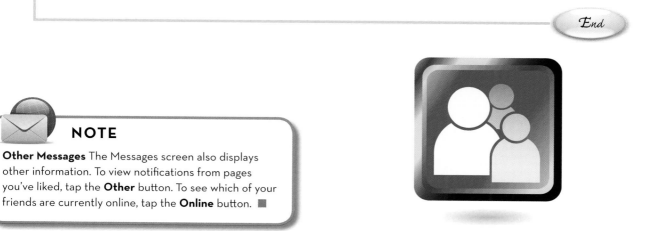

### NOTE

**Other Messages** The Messages screen also displays other information. To view notifications from pages you've liked, tap the **Other** button. To see which of your friends are currently online, tap the **Online** button. ■

# CHATTING WITH FRIENDS

If you need to send an instant message to one of your Facebook friends, you can do that from your iPhone, too. All you have to do is access Facebook's mobile chat feature.

*Start*

Tap the **Menu** button on the Facebook toolbar to display the Home screen.

Scroll down to the Apps section and tap **Chat**.

*Continued*

**3** You now see a list of friends who are currently online. Tap a person's name to initiate a chat session.

**4** Use the onscreen keyboard to enter your initial message.

**5** Tap the **Send** button.

**6** Your ongoing conversation displays in the top of the window.

*End*

**TIP**

**Green Dots** Friends who are available for chat have a green dot next to their names in the chat list. ■

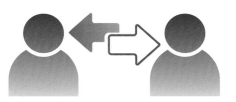

# Glossary

## A

**activity log**   A tool, accessed from the timeline page, that lets users view and manage all past Facebook activity.

**album**   A collection of photos or videos, organized around a user-created theme.

**app**   Short for *application*, a utility, service, or game that runs from within the Facebook website and shares users' Facebook data.

## B

**blog**   A website where the host records his or her personal opinions and information in the form of short "stories" or posts.

**browser**   A program, such as Internet Explorer, that displays web pages, such as Facebook.

## C

**CAPTCHA**   A rather tortured acronym for "Completely Automated Public Turing test to tell Computers and Humans Apart," this is a text-based challenge-response test used to ensure a response is generated from a real human being and not a machine or software program.

**chat**   On Facebook, a feature that lets users send text-based instant messages to each other.

**Chat pane**   The pane on the right side of the Facebook window that displays online friends available for chat.

**comment**   A response to a Facebook status update, photo, video, or other item.

**cover**   The large image displayed across the top of a Facebook timeline page.

**crop**   To cut off or mask the unwanted parts of an image.

## D

**deactivate** (account)   To temporarily suspend the use of a Facebook account. Deactivated accounts can be reactivated.

**delete** (account)   To permanently remove a Facebook account. Deleted accounts cannot be reactivated.

## E

**email**   Electronic mail; a means of corresponding with other computer users over the Internet through digital messages. Facebook assigns users their own facebook.com email addresses.

**event**   On Facebook, any public or private gathering that is publicized via the Facebook site to one's Facebook friends.

## F

**face recognition**   Technology that identifies faces in photographic images. Facebook uses face recognition technology to suggest tags in photos users upload to the site.

**Facebook**   The Internet's largest social network.

**friend**   On Facebook, a person you agree to connect to and share information with. As a verb, one can *friend* other users on the Facebook site.

**friend request**   The invitation to become a friend of another Facebook user. Both users must agree to be friends before the friend connection is established.

**friends list**   One's master list of Facebook friends. Facebook also lets you organize your friends into smaller, more targeted lists, which are also called friends lists.

## G

**Google+**   Google's social network.

## H

**home page**   On Facebook, the very first page on the site that typically displays the user's news feed after logging in.

## I–J

**icon**   A graphic symbol that represents a location or action on the Facebook site.

**inbox**   The primary folder in which incoming email and other messages are stored.

**instant messaging**   Text-based, real-time one-on-one communication over the Internet.

**Internet**   The global network of networks that connects millions of computers and other devices around the world.

**iPhone**   Apple's popular smartphone.

## K–L

**life event**   A major turning point in one's life, as noted on the Facebook timeline.

**lightbox**   The photo and video viewer on the Facebook site.

**like**   The option to acknowledge a status update or other item in a news feed in a positive fashion.

**LinkedIn**   A social network dedicated to and used primarily by business professionals.

## M–N

**message**   On the Facebook site, any private communication between users.

**micro-blogging service**   An online service, such as Twitter, that exists solely to broadcast short text posts from users to groups of followers.

**navigation sidebar**   The sidebar or panel on the left side of most Facebook pages that contains links to other pages and services on the site.

**news feed**   The continuous list of status updates from your Facebook friends and pages you like, as displayed on a Facebook user's home page.

**notifications**   Notices from Facebook regarding important activity.

## O–P

**Open Graph**   Facebook's protocol that enables the connection to and sharing of data with third-party websites and services.

**Page**   The Facebook presence of public figures, celebrities, companies, and brands. Facebook Pages can be liked or subscribed to, which is the equivalent of friending these entities.

**Password**   A series of letters, numbers, and symbols used to log in to your Facebook account.

**Pinterest**   A social network built on the "pinning" of images to virtual pinboards.

**post**   As a noun, another word for a Facebook status update. As a verb, the act of creating said status update.

**Privacy button**   The button found next to all new status updates and many account settings that lets users determine who can view that particular item.

**privacy settings**   Those settings on the Facebook site that determine who can view a particular piece of information.

**profile**   Your collection of personal information on the Facebook site, as displayed on the timeline page.

**profile picture**   The personal photograph or image you choose to display on your timeline page and next to all your status updates.

**Publisher box**   The text box into which you enter new status updates.

## Q-R

**question**    On Facebook, a query or poll that one asks to those on his friends list.

**recent stories**    In the Facebook news feed, those status updates most recently posted by friends.

**resolution**    The degree of clarity displayed in a photographic or video image, typically expressed by the number of horizontal and vertical pixels.

## S

**smart list**    A friends list created automatically by Facebook. The three default smart lists are Close Friends, Acquaintances, and Family; Facebook also generates smart lists for one's current places of employment and education.

**smartphone**    A mobile phone with Internet connectivity and a web browser built in, such as the Apple iPhone.

**social ad**    An advertisement on the Facebook site that references friends who like or use the advertiser's services or products.

**social bookmarking services**    Sites such as Digg and Delicious that let users share their favorite web pages with friends and colleagues online.

**social game**    A game played on a social networking site, typically with or against other users of that network.

**social media**    Online media (websites, blogs, and so on) designed for social interaction.

**social network**    A website or service designed to facilitate the sharing of items and information between members.

**status update**    On Facebook, a public message posted to other users.

**story**    Another name for a Facebook status update.

**subscribe**    The process of signing up to receive a Facebook member's status updates without necessarily becoming a formal friend.

## T-U-V

**tag**    The process of identifying a Facebook member in a photo or video.

**thumbnail**    A smaller version of a larger picture, typically used for quick identification purposes.

**ticker**    The real-time flow of member activity displayed in the top right corner on your Facebook home page.

**timeline**    A user's collection of status updates, photos, videos, and life events, arranged in chronological order as a Facebook profile.

**toolbar**    The strip of icons/buttons at the top of every Facebook page that lead to further locations and actions.

**top stories**    The most important status updates from your friends, as determined by Facebook.

**Twitter**    A popular micro-blogging service, where users post 140-character (maximum) *tweets* to their followers.

**unfriend**    The process of removing a user from your Facebook friends list.

**URL (uniform resource locator)**    The address that identifies a web page to a browser. Also known as a *web address*.

**video chat**    Facebook's real-time webcam-based communication.

## W-X-Y-Z

**web address**    See *URL*.

**web link**    A link to a web page.

**web page**    An HTML file, containing text, graphics, and even mini-applications, viewed with a web browser.

**webcam**    A small video camera connected to a computer.

**website**    An organized, linked collection of web pages stored on an Internet server and read using a web browser.

**YouTube**    The Internet's largest video-sharing community.

**Zuckerberg, Mark**    The founder of Facebook.

# Index

# G

# X-Y-Z

# MAKE THE MOST OF YOUR SMARTPHONE, TABLET, COMPUTER, AND MORE! CHECK OUT THE MY... BOOK SERIES

ISBN 13: 9780789750334     ISBN 13: 9780789748515     ISBN 13: 9780789749482     ISBN 13: 9780789749819

## Full-Color, Step-by-Step Guides

The "My..." series is a visually rich, task-based series to help you get up and running with your new device and technology, and tap into some of the hidden, or less obvious, features. The organized, task-based format allows you to quickly and easily find exactly the task you want to accomplish, and then shows you how to achieve it with minimal text and plenty of visual cues.

**Visit quepublishing.com/mybooks to learn more about the My... book series from Que.**